THE
DREAM
THAT WILL NOT DIE

Books by Charles Paul Conn:

The Possible Dream
The Winners Circle
An Uncommon Freedom
Promises to Keep
Believe! (with Richard M. DeVos)
FatherCare
No Easy Game (with Terry Bradshaw)
Julian Carroll of Kentucky
The New Johnny Cash
The Barbara Mandrell Story
Hooked on a Good Thing (with Sammy Hall)
Making it Happen
Eckerd: The Right Prescription (with Jack Eckerd)
Kathy (with Barbara Miller)
The Power of Positive Students (with William Mitchell)
Just Off Chicken Street (with Floyd McClung Jr.)
Disguised (with Patricia Moore)
The Magnificent Three (with Nicky Cruz)
Battle for Africa (with Brother Andrew)
Dad, Mom, and the Church

THE
DREAM
THAT WILL NOT DIE

Charles Paul Conn

Commonwealth Books
66 Charles Street
Boston, MA 02114

Portions of the material in chapter 1 are adapted from
The Possible Dream with permission from Fleming H.
Revell Company, Grand Rapids, Michigan.

Photos used by permission from
Amway Corporation and InterNET.

*This book is dedicated
to the memory of
MELODY.
Our love for her,
our memories of her
will never die.*

Hold fast to dreams,
For if dreams die,
Life is a broken-winged bird
That cannot fly.

— Langston Hughes

Contents

Publisher's Introduction

Rarely in American history has a new business created shock waves equal to that of Amway. One business expert has called it "the most hotly discussed and least understood national corporation in this century."

Since the company was launched fewer than forty years ago, it has rocketed to the top of the huge direct-sales industry and shows no signs of slowing. And the Amway phenomenon is no longer a purely American one; the company is now one of the five largest U.S. exporters to Japan, operates in more than seventy countries, and is growing at breathtaking speed in Latin America and the new markets of formerly communist Eastern Europe.

Despite its dramatic success — or perhaps because of it —

the company still remains something of a mystery to the general public. The name *Amway* is such a household word that it appears in the novels of Stephen King, the stand-up comedy routines of David Letterman and Jay Leno, and the dialogue of popular movies. Everyone, it seems, has heard of Amway.

Still, for all its familiarity, most people know little about it, who runs it, or how it works. One reason for the confusion is that Amway itself is rapidly evolving; as a business concept, it is a "work in progress," to a degree, and what was true about Amway twenty years ago may not be valid today.

Another reason is that Amway itself is practiced in a hundred different ways around the world, depending on the regional culture and the personalities of different frontline leaders who reinvent the business according to their own philosophies. This is an inherent part of the Amway system itself. It encourages, or at least permits, the business to change in the hands of dozens of independent entrepreneurs, some of whom manage it better than others, and all of whom inject into it their own styles.

To the general public, of course, this can be confusing. In the cookie-cutter environment of the 1990s, one McDonald's restaurant looks and operates like any other McDonald's, and every Hilton hotel is a virtual clone of every other. In such a franchise-crazy world, people assume that the Amway business they saw last year in Omaha is exactly like the one they see this year in Kokomo. With hamburgers and hotel rooms, maybe so; but Amway is a more complex and subtle business than that. If you've seen one distributorship, you have *not* necessarily seen them all.

Many people have analyzed Amway in the news media. It has been the subject of numerous books, magazine articles, and television reports. Dozens of writers have attempted to explain this unusual business but none more effectively, or with greater commercial success, than award-winning author Charles Paul Conn.

Conn was the first freelance writer to reach a national audience with the story of what he called "the Amway experience." He is a popular writer who had earlier coauthored books with such celebrities as country singer Johnny Cash and pro football star Terry Bradshaw. Conn discovered Amway when he was invited by founding president Rich DeVos to coauthor a book with him in 1975. The book was titled *Believe!* and was an instant success. Afterwards, Conn wrote a cover article on DeVos for the *Saturday Evening Post* and authored a book on Amway itself in 1977.

Conn's book, *The Possible Dream,* became an international sensation. It reached the Top Ten list of *Time* magazine, made the Top Ten charts of every major big-city newspaper in America, and was featured on the *New York Times* best-seller list for three straight months. *Publishers Weekly,* the trade journal of the American book industry, officially declared it the No. 7 best-selling hardcover book in the U.S. for all of 1977. It sold millions of copies in English, was translated into other languages, and eventually became the blockbuster best-selling corporate biography in American publishing history with eight million copies printed to date.

With the success of *The Possible Dream,* Conn was recognized by the media as the nation's most credible expert on the subject of Amway and its unique corporate culture. He wrote a series of books on the subject during the next few years, all of them best-sellers, appeared on dozens of talk shows and radio/TV call-ins, and was interviewed by media leaders ranging from Larry King to the *New York Times.*

Conn's reporting on Amway in books and interviews was a critical element in the company's rise to national prominence during the late 1970s and early 1980s. Conn was given credit for identifying the young company as a major market force long before others in the national press did so and for shaping public opinion about it in a positive direction at a pivotal time.

As a journalist constantly asked to analyze and explain Amway, Conn has sought to retain his objectivity by maintaining an arm's-length relationship with the company. He has never been an employee of Amway Corporation or an Amway distributor, and his purposeful detachment has preserved his widespread credibility in discussing Amway with the general public.

In 1986, Conn withdrew from his career as a freelance writer to accept the presidency of Lee College, a liberal arts college in Tennessee that is his alma mater. (Conn earned a doctorate in psychology from Emory University and served as a postdoctoral scholar at Harvard University.) He explains his decision to lead Lee College as "a matter of the heart," and during his ten years as president he has, until now, declined to write any book-length projects for national distribution.

In 1996, Conn again tackles the difficult subject of Amway, which continues to intrigue both him and the public globally. "It is a new day, and it is a new Amway," he explains. "It is time once again to write about what Amway is and what it is *not*." In this contemporary treatment, which draws upon his earlier work to describe the origins of the company, Conn focuses on one particular group of Amway distributors to illustrate how the world of Amway operates.

Readers will find it a fascinating story, told in Conn's trademark style: clear and memorable, never distorting the simple facts. He lays out the personalities and events and lets them speak for themselves. We think a new audience, like millions of readers before, will enjoy the way he tells the rest of the Amway story.

The Publishers

1

Partners

Amway started with a handshake deal between two teenagers. Jay Van Andel and Rich DeVos were schoolboys at Grand Rapids Christian School. Rich was fourteen years old and had no car; he disliked riding the bus to school and back each day. He noticed that the sixteen-year-old Jay had a car and drove to school alone.

Rich made Jay an offer: If I pay you twenty-five cents each week for gas, will you give me a ride to school each day? It made sense to the older Van Andel, and a deal was struck. It was 1940.

The year 1940 was a year so remote from the 1990s that it seems another world.

In 1940 Adolf Hitler's German army invaded Holland,

Belgium, and France, sweeping through to Paris as fast as their panzer tanks could carry them.

The year 1940 was also the year that *Gone With the Wind* won an armful of Oscars at the Academy Awards ceremonies, and the lines of people waiting to see the movie grew even longer. The helicopter was developed that year; its first flight lasted a full fifteen minutes. Nylon stockings were placed on sale for the first time; women stormed the counters of clothing stores in every major city, and even with a two-pair-per-customer limit, the entire supply of seventy-two thousand pairs in New York City sold out in eight hours. The Cincinnati Reds, on the strong pitching of Johnny VanderMeer, beat the Detroit Tigers in a seven-game World Series at old Crosley Field in what was still the American pastime of baseball. And in a somewhat more serious contest, Franklin D. Roosevelt audaciously ran for an unprecedented third term as president and clobbered Republican Wendell Willkie at the polls.

Gasoline cost ten cents a gallon. The Golden Gate Bridge, a new attraction for San Francisco gawkers, was just completed; television was still a laboratory fantasy; and Joe Louis was in his early prime, virtually unchallenged in boxing as heavyweight champion of the world.

It was also in 1940 that a serious young teenager at a Christian high school in Grand Rapids, Michigan, became the owner of his first car. The student was Jay Van Andel. He came from a large Dutch community in Grand Rapids. For years Van Andel had ridden a bicycle to school — quite a distance from the south side of town — because it was important to him that he attend the school, which is owned and operated by members of the Christian Reformed Church. But winters can be rough on bicyclists in Grand Rapids, and when his family moved to the north side of town — to a neighborhood even farther from the school — his father bought him an old Model A Ford.

Enter Rich DeVos. "I didn't know him," Van Andel recalls, "but I had noticed him before. He was in one of my classes, and for some reason I remember being aware of him and being attracted to him." DeVos made his offer: "*Your* car, *my* gas money." It was a good deal for both boys. DeVos, who had been riding the bus every day, now had transportation; and Van Andel, who had paid the cost of driving alone, now had a partner.

The arrangement they made that day was a good one; and today, half a century later, Jay Van Andel and Rich DeVos are still riding side-by-side, not as passengers in a Model A Ford, but as founders of Amway Corporation.

Amway is one of America's most intriguing companies and surely one of the most interesting stories of partnership and success in recent economic history. Since 1940, the battles of World War II, Korea, and Vietnam have been fought; eleven different presidents have occupied the White House; *Gone With the Wind* has gone and returned again; nylon stockings have given way to panty hose; Crosley Field has been replaced by Riverfront Stadium; and Joe Louis has watched from ringside as the likes of Marciano, Ali, and Tyson have fought for his crown.

But a few things have endured. The Golden Gate Bridge hasn't changed. Helicopters and television are still around. And Rich DeVos and Jay Van Andel have endured — not merely endured but prospered, not only individually, but together, as a team. Operating with a finely tuned communication which only they understand, the partners jointly created one of the world's largest privately owned companies, with little more than a handshake and a gentleman's agreement. It is more than one could have expected from two teenage buddies driving to school together every morning in a Model A Ford.

* * * * *

Rich DeVos is fond of saying that men make very few big decisions in life, that strings of small, insignificant decisions usually carry them in the paths their lives take.

His own liaison with Jay Van Andel over the years is a perfect example of his point. From their first agreement to share a ride to school, the friendship grew by small steps, finally becoming a relationship of enormous importance, directly affecting hundreds of thousands of people and billions of dollars each year. The two men are, in a sense, inextricably bound to one another by a web of circumstance and shared interests. They are the ultimate example of businessmen-partners, and much is made of the rare way in which they complemented one another — the remarkable degree to which their separate skills and inclinations meshed in an efficient working whole. But it is important to remember that they were not selected for one another by a computer, each chosen for the way his own set of counterbalancing qualities fit the other. They did not set out with calculating forethought to put together a two-man executive superteam, though it worked out that way. In the beginning they were just two schoolboys who enjoyed being together. "Sometimes people forget," Van Andel says, "that Rich and I got together because we liked each other. That's all. We became partners simply because we liked each other. We enjoyed being together."

When World War II engulfed the United States, DeVos and Van Andel both enlisted for military service. Both entered the Army Air Corps and served until the end of the war. They stayed in touch during their years of service, and on one occasion they were home on leave at the same time. It was then that they first talked seriously about going into business together after the war.

One Sunday night, just before each was to leave Grand

Rapids to return to duty, they sat up late at night, talked about the future, and agreed to open "some sort of business" together.

"Some sort of business" turned out to be the Wolverine Air Service, a flying school and air charter service at Comstock Park, near Grand Rapids. Van Andel was discharged from the Corps several months before DeVos, so he took the lead in establishing the business. DeVos, still overseas, wrote his father and asked him to give Van Andel seven hundred dollars — his total savings — for half the start-up cost of the business.

By the time DeVos returned to Grand Rapids, the flying school was almost ready to operate. DeVos remembers: "We hit a snag. When we got our customers signed up and our instructors hired, we discovered the runways at the little airport had not been completed yet. They were still nothing but giant streaks of mud. We improvised. A river ran alongside the airport, so we bought some floats for our Piper Cub and flew right off the water, taking off and landing on those pontoon floats. We were supposed to have offices there at the little airstrip, but they weren't built in time for our opening. Jay bought a chicken coop from a farmer down the road, hauled it over to the airstrip, whitewashed it, and hung a sign that read grandly: WOLVERINE AIR SERVICE. We were in business."

One thing led to another. The partners, apparently concluding that the aviation business left them with too much idle time on their hands, opened a hamburger stand in a prefab building that they erected at the airstrip. It had a one-man kitchen and space around it for cars to park — an early Grand Rapids version of what would later be called a "drive-in restaurant." On opening day the power company reported they couldn't deliver electricity on schedule, so the rookie restaurateurs rented a portable generator and opened on time anyway. The division of labor was simple:

DeVos grilled hamburgers while Van Andel "hopped" cars or Van Andel did the burgers while DeVos did the cars. It worked out about the same either way. Both remember the restaurant experience with a conspicuous lack of enthusiasm.

After two years, they sold the businesses for a tidy profit and decided it was time to reward themselves for their hard work with a bit of adventure on the high seas. They got just a bit more adventure than they had planned.

They pooled their money and sank it into an old thirty-eight-foot schooner called *Elizabeth*. In December of 1948, they set sail from Norwalk, Connecticut, for a year-long cruise in the Atlantic Ocean. They planned to sail down the East Coast of the United States, through the Caribbean, and eventually down the coast of South America. They were going to learn to sail as they went, of course, since neither of them had ever been sailing on a boat before!

Van Andel and DeVos learned fast. In a few weeks they were sailing and navigating with a reasonable amount of skill, but as luck would have it, by the time they finally learned what they were doing, the *Elizabeth* began to leak. One dark night in March as they sailed from Havana, bound for Haiti, the leaky, old hull finally gave up the ghost, and the schooner sank in fifteen hundred feet of water, ten miles off the northern coast of Cuba. The two sailors were rescued by an American freighter called the *Addabell Lydes,* which dropped them off a few days later in San Juan, Puerto Rico.

Both men vow that it never seriously occurred to them to turn back. They wired home to assure their parents they were safe and to arrange to collect insurance benefits on their ill-fated schooner, then struck out again. They spent five months traveling through the islands and went on to Central and South America before finally their vacation ended, and they returned to Grand Rapids.

By the time they got home, they were hungry again, not for adventure this time, but for achievement — for accomplishments of substance and permanence. They went into business together again the very month they returned from South America, and this time their focus was a business which would last a lifetime.

* * * * *

It was a visit from a distant relative that got DeVos and Van Andel started in business. The relative was a second cousin of Van Andel's, a fiftyish Dutch immigrant named Neil Maaskant. He lived in Chicago, and he called to tell cousin Jay that he had started a new business, asking if he could drive up to Grand Rapids to talk about it.

It was August 1949. The two friends had just returned from South America and were ready to settle down and work, so the timing was right for them. "Sure, why not?" they answered. It couldn't hurt to hear what he had to say.

One night they talked until after 2:00 A.M. When the visitor finally departed, the names of Rich DeVos and Jay Van Andel were on the dotted line at the bottom of an application form. They were distributors of a line of food supplements called Nutrilite Products.

Nutrilite Products was a California-based direct-sales company. *Direct sales* meant simply that its foods were marketed by individual distributors who sold directly to their customers.

A direct-sales business may not have been exactly what the two partners were looking for, but when the Nutrilite sales plan was explained, it sounded easy enough to them. Maaskant had shown them his commission check, and it was a hefty amount. They reasoned that if he, a middle-aged immigrant with a still-thick Dutch accent, could make big money in this business, certainly they could do as well. So they signed up. The product they were selling was a box of Nutrilite food supplement capsules, a month's supply costing $19.50, and the next day they sold to their first customer. "He was an old man who ran a beer-and-wine, pick-up grocery on the lake nearby," DeVos recalls. "We asked him to buy a box and he did, just because he liked us. After we made that one sale, we didn't do another thing for two weeks."

The Nutrilite business was a fairly simple one. A distributor gave a friend or neighbor a copy of a booklet entitled *How to Get Well and Stay Well,* which described the need for food supplements, or perhaps made an appointment to give a presentation personally. If the distributor could convince the individual of the need for a dietary supplement, he made a customer of him, supplying him with a box of food supplement tablets (Nutrilite "XX") each month for $19.50. The system in those days required new distributors to sell products to twenty-five customers before they were eligible to sponsor other distributors.

Van Andel and DeVos worked hard, and their business grew rapidly. Within several months they had built one of the most successful distributorships in the Nutrilite business.

It wasn't all smooth water. They held their first public meeting for prospective distributors in the basement of a little restaurant at the Grand Rapids airport. They had placed an ad in the paper and hoped for a hundred people. Only eight people showed. All eight came together, marched to the front row, and sat down. Jay gave a little welcoming speech and showed a film about nutrition, then Rich gave a closing pitch and invited "all who were interested" to stay and talk over the business. All eight people stood up and marched out. They didn't say hello, goodbye, boo or kiss-my-foot. They just walked out.

About five minutes later, as the two partners were glumly packing up their projector and sales material, one of the eight came back in the door. "My wife made me come back to explain to you guys," he said. "We are in the Nutrilite business already, and we just wanted to see what you young fellows were up to." And with that he was gone. That discouraged them even more. They hadn't known anyone else was selling Nutrilite in the Grand Rapids area, and they wondered whether or not there would be room for them to build their business in the same town.

There were good days, too. Outstanding distributors started coming out of the woodwork, providing leadership of their own, widening the circle of contacts. They opened a small office on Eastern Avenue in Grand Rapids. New people began to come aboard who would stay for a lifetime. One was a barber named Fred Hansen who was from Akron, Ohio, and who started a strong distributorship there. Fred Hansen's widow, Bernice, remembers those early days: "We were back in Grand Rapids visiting when Fred heard about a new business and went to a meeting to hear about it. He came back, and I asked what it was all about. 'Selling pills door-to-door,' he said. That sounded terrible. But a month later he learned more about it and got in. We were living in Akron, and Rich DeVos drove all the way from Grand Rapids — 325 miles — in an old Packard automobile. We had five couples there. I made a coffee cake and sent the kids upstairs, and Rich held the meeting. All five of those couples came into the business that night, and before he left, Rich reminded me that the money I had spent on the coffee cake was tax-deductible!" That was June of 1950.

Van Andel and DeVos were young and aggressive. As the business gathered momentum, they pushed even harder. People like Joe Victor, a milk-truck driver, built large distributorships rapidly, setting an example that motivated others. One distributor from those early days tells about becoming concerned when his sales volume dropped slightly one month. He wrote DeVos to complain about the distributors in his organization not working. He got a terse note back in reply: "Start working harder yourself, and you'll set a better example." But if the two young entrepreneurs accepted few excuses from their distributors, they also maintained a high standard for themselves.

DeVos reminisces about what it was like in those days. "I remember one night in Lansing, Michigan, Jay and I had a big sales meeting. It was really going to be a dandy! We had been on radio with big ads and had put notices in the paper. All day long we collared people and passed out brochures, revving up for a big meeting. We had an auditorium with two hundred seats, and that night two people showed up! Did you ever make a rock-'em-sock-'em sales pitch to two people in a room with two hundred seats? And then drive home at two o'clock in the morning because you couldn't afford to pay the motel rates? You do one of two things: either you give up or you persist. We persisted."

Unfortunately, things began to go badly for Nutrilite on a national scale. The problem was one of internal warfare. The company was actually two companies: Nutrilite Products, Incorporated, which made the products, and Mytinger and Casselberry, which operated the distributor organization. The two companies had worked well together for years but began to quarrel over many different problems. Eventually the bickering erupted into full-scale warfare.

DeVos and Van Andel decided that the Nutrilite situation was too precarious to depend on. Nutrilite or no Nutrilite, they had a group of distributors to whom they felt responsible, many of whom had left their jobs to go full-time. If Nutrilite couldn't provide the leadership to keep those distributors healthy, then it was the responsibility of Van Andel and DeVos to move into the vacuum and lead the way. In the summer of 1958, at a meeting of their leading distributors in Charlevoix, Michigan, they made their announcement: We intend to develop our own product line. We will continue to sell Nutrilite products, but we can no longer depend solely on that company to supply our distributorships with marketable products. It is up to us to make our own way.

With that explanation, the two partners gave the people in their group the opportunity to stay with them or to remain entirely with Nutrilite. To a person, the leaders at Charlevoix chose to head into new territory with DeVos and Van Andel.

That meeting marked the cutting of the umbilical cord which tied the small group to Nutrilite exclusively. A few months later, in early 1959, DeVos and Van Andel sat in the basement office of Jay's home in Ada, Michigan, and officially organized Amway Corporation. It was a bold, hopeful beginning — a gamble that they could make it alone and build an organization of size and permanence. Today, one can easily see that it was the start of something big. At the time, one couldn't be so sure.

* * * * *

Their biggest challenge at the outset was to develop a product line. They had experimented with a few household items and believed that the best products for a direct sales organization were everyday commodities — soaps, detergents, and household and personal-care products. In the next few years, they tested their notion by occasionally introducing big-ticket items into the product line (even fallout shelters!) and always returned to their original view that household products were best suited to the Amway marketing system.

A tube of toothpaste is easy to sell. Everyone uses it. It runs out and must be replaced, creating the opportunity for repeat business. And, most importantly, it requires no specialized training to sell. One needs no technical expertise to explain to a customer how to operate a bar of soap. There is no installation-and-maintenance problem with a tube of lipstick. "Why do we sell soap?" DeVos asked in his speeches. "Because people buy soap!"

Van Andel explained, "We wanted to provide an opportunity that virtually any hardworking person could take advantage of. With household products, the new distributor doesn't have the task of creating a demand for the product, of convincing the customer that he needs it. The demand is already there. All the distributor must do is say, 'Look, you're buying this product at the supermarket already. I want to offer you a product as good or better at a comparable price, and I'll bring it to your door, give you individual service, and guarantee your money back if you're not satisfied.' Now that's not a bad deal. That is the kind of sales that anyone can do. Household products fit into our concept of a sort of 'Everyman' business, as opposed to a business for big-ticket, supersalesman types."

The first product to be sold in volume by the new company was a liquid all-purpose cleanser called Frisk. It was an unusually effective cleaning liquid and became the first product on the Amway list; a successor to that product still is a staple of the product line, now bearing the name L.O.C. (for "liquid organic concentrate"). Soon after, they introduced a dry-compound laundry detergent called *S-A-8*, which is also near the top of the list in sales volume among Amway products today.

As the Amway product line increased, DeVos and Van Andel would eventually buy out their suppliers and bring the manufacturing process to Grand Rapids. They had learned from the Nutrilite experience that quality control of their products was critically important and determined to make their own products as soon as possible.

Meanwhile, the growth of the distributor force continued.

DeVos and Van Andel had bought property on a hill over-looking the Thornapple River in a community called Ada and built homes near one another on that hill. The new Amway Corporation began operating in those houses, with the basements being made into offices. At first, the team consisted only of the two men and their wives, with office help being added as the operation grew.

And grow it did. The DeVos-Van Andel combination was a potent force. They worked as if their lives depended on it. Sponsor. Train. Motivate. It has always been the same formula. In the early days, Van Andel did most of the spon-soring of new distributors, and DeVos directed the sales force as it was built. They would go into a town — any-where within a few hundred miles of Ada — and place ads in the paper, make contact with prospects in their homes, hold a meeting in a motel room or a rented hall of some sort, and sponsor new distributors.

In 1960, a seventeen-year-old kid named Wally Buttrick made extra money mowing lawns in Ada. He was an ambi-tious kid who went around the community knocking on doors, asking for business. One day he knocked on the door of a house on Windy Hill, and Jay Van Andel answered. Buttrick began mowing the Van Andel lawn for one dollar an hour. He was curious about the office opera-tion that was going on so furiously inside, and when he inquired about it, Van Andel offered him a job running the mimeograph machine and putting addresses on envelopes. He helped assemble the first eighteen-page career manual, collating the pages on the basement Ping-Pong table.

"Jay was amazing," Van Andel recalls. "He could write all this stuff, then go to the typewriter and type it himself, then run it off on the mimeograph machine, then help put it together and staple it. He was a one-man army." And while Van Andel was managing that, DeVos was running the sales operation. If someone came to Ada to pick up an order, he would go to the basement office, check the order, jump in his car and drive to the warehouse they had rented nearby, fill the order, and put it in the fellow's car for him.

The fledgling Amway operation necessarily involved Betty Van Andel and Helen DeVos. Both wives had the task of maintaining a normal home life for young children while their husbands conducted the bustling distributor activity literally under their feet. The key roles the two wives played set a pattern that continues in Amway today of husbands and wives working together as a team.

After a year, they moved out of the basement office. They bought an old gas station, forty by sixty feet, in Ada and put their first office and a small print shop there. It was the first of literally scores of construction projects that would occur during the next four decades. Two months after moving into the gas station, a fifty-six-hundred-square-foot manufacturing facility was added. The next year there were six new building projects; then a tank farm was added, plus a warehouse and a servicing area for the truck fleet. The office and manufacturing space was enlarged three times. In 1964 came three more warehouses, a cluster of storage silos, a twenty-thousand-square-foot administration building, and five other expansion projects. And on and on. Explosive growth each year: A railroad spur, two hangars at the Kent County Airport, and other buildings of almost every description.

The present Amway facility occupies a three-hundred-acre tract, with more than one million square feet under roof at Ada, with another half-million square feet in seven regional distribution centers around the country — all from that forty-by-sixty building in 1960!

Those buildings weren't being built just to keep the construction industry healthy. The expansion was forced by a soaring sales volume, which was in turn produced by the growing distributor force. "Those guys worked hard," an

Ada resident says. "Every night you could go by there and see the lights on 'til 2:00 or 3:00 A.M." Buttrick graduated from errand-boy status to assisting DeVos on the road. "We started going to places too far away to drive, so they rented a used single-engine plane from a guy who owned a dry-cleaning shop. Later they got a twin-engine Piper, then a Beechcraft. We went all over the country in that thing. It was lots of work, but things were growing so fast, and we had fun, too."

The meteoric development of Amway from that tiny beginning to its present size ranks among the most impressive success stories in recent corporate history.

There have been many factors which have spurred Amway's growth, but the primary ingredient of the company's success may have been an attitude, more than the marketing plan or the economic climate. A friend recalls driving past the Amway plant late one night in the early 1960s. It was a chilly night, about 11:30 P.M., and he was surprised to see Rich DeVos and Jay Van Andel on the front lawn, digging a hole in which to erect a sign that lay nearby. "What in the world are you fellows doing *that* for?" he asked incredulously. They paused in their digging. One of them looked up at him, grinned, and said, "Well, what's the use in paying somebody else to do something you can do yourself?"

They had a dream, and they were willing to work for it.

2

Amway Today

That was then. This is now. The Amway that started as a basement business in 1959 is the same Amway that today ranks as one of the largest direct-sales companies in the world with more than six billion dollars in annual sales. In nearly four decades, the little Michigan soap company has become a global giant.

The sheer size is impressive.

There are now 2.5 million Amway distributors operating in seventy-plus countries and territories around the world. To supply these distributors, thirteen thousand employees work in manufacturing, corporate headquarters, and offices around the globe. A massive fleet of tractor-trailer rigs runs around the clock to shuttle products from the Michigan manufacturing plant to nine regional distribution centers across the United States and throughout the dozens of countries where Amway operates.

The products themselves are more diversified than even DeVos and Van Andel could have dreamed when they began with their first cleaning concentrate. More than four hundred products carry the Amway name, and a three-hundred-plus page *Personal Shoppers Catalog*® gives access to another menu of sixty-five hundred brand-name items. Amway distributors also sell such services as MCI long-distance calling and the like. And the numbers on these bigger-ticket items are astounding: As one example, the Amway Water Treatment System® sold more than 450,000 units in 1995 alone!

Amway's growth curve is climbing more steeply in the mid-1990s than at any time in its history. The increase in retail sales for 1995 was 19 percent; the year before that, it was 18 percent; and the year before that, 20 percent.

All of this has been accomplished with little corporate debt. The conservative spending habits of the founders' Dutch ancestry are reflected in the Amway balance sheet, and the founders have built more than ten million square feet of factories and office facilities with little borrowing. Even among their overseas affiliates, the numbers are rock solid. For instance, in Japan alone, a recent government filing shows the company held $750 million in cash assets with no debt.

Such tremendous success shows in the way Amway operates. The company owns a private resort, Peter Island, in the British Virgin Islands, complete with yacht club and luxury hotel. It maintains a fleet of jet airplanes — ten, at last count — ranging from a small Lear to a customized 727. Its ocean-going yachts, each dubbed *Enterprise,* have hauled successful distributors around the Mediterranean and Caribbean for years. It owns the largest convention hotel in western Michigan, the Amway Grand Plaza Hotel in Grand Rapids.

Most of these corporate luxuries are used for training and rewards for the distributors themselves. Amway maintains a fiercely distributor-centered strategy. Virtually every aspect of company policy is designed to provide career development for successful distributors. The island, the yachts and airplanes, and other Amway holdings are maintained to improve distributor performance. Van Andel and DeVos, who were once themselves distributors, have not forgotten that the motor that makes Amway run is the distributors' confidence that the company will invest its resources to train whoever creates business at the retail level.

* * * * *

As massive as the company has become, perhaps the greatest miracle of the Amway story is that it has retained its status as a private, family-owned corporation. Rich and Jay have each stepped down from active management of the company and watch from a distance as their children lead the business on a day-to-day basis.

DeVos was first to retire from his role as co-CEO. He underwent heart bypass surgery — his second — in early 1993 and stepped down at the age of sixty-seven. Dick DeVos, his oldest son, assumed the presidency at that time, at the age of thirty-one. Van Andel followed suit two years later, leaving his post as chairman to be filled by Steve Van Andel, also an oldest son.

In 1996, the second-generation Van Andel and DeVos operate as partners and co-CEOs just as their fathers did. All the other children, three from each family, serve in the corporate structure. Doug (senior vice president and managing director of North America), Dan, and Cheri DeVos Vander Weide join with Dave (senior vice president of operations), Nan, and Barb Van Andel-Gaby to round out the family leadership team.

The two families retain not just control but actual ownership of the company. For a six-billion-dollar company to be wholly owned by two families is virtually unheard of in the American corporate world today, but the DeVos and Van Andel families have managed somehow to finance the company's meteoric growth without selling it off piece by piece.

The families have sold shares only in Amway affiliates in Asian markets. A minority percentage of Amway Japan Ltd. is available to the public on the New York Stock Exchange, as is a percentage of Amway Asia Pacific Ltd., which includes China and other markets.

Otherwise, it all belongs to the two Grand Rapids schoolboys who shared the ride in that Model A Ford long ago. The obvious question is often asked: How wealthy *are* they? No one knows for sure, maybe not even DeVos and Van Andel themselves, but the best educated guess probably comes from *Forbes* magazine, which works hard to calculate such things. *Forbes* pegs the net worth of each partner at four billion dollars, give or take a few hundred million. *Fortune* magazine has recently offered a similar estimate and lists each man separately as among the ten wealthiest individuals in America.

In addition to their ownership of Amway Corporation, both families have diversified into other holdings. Most highly publicized of these ventures is the ownership by the DeVos family of the Orlando Magic, the professional basketball team which in 1995 stopped just one round short of winning the championship of the National Basketball Association (NBA). The Magic roster currently includes such superstar celebrities as Shaquille "Shaq" O'Neal and Anfernee "Penny" Hardaway, and owning the team has brought considerable publicity, almost all of it positive, to DeVos.

"It's an interesting thing," he commented recently, "I

have been the president of an international corporation for more than thirty years, and no one notices. Then I buy one little basketball team, and suddenly people in airports are recognizing me because I'm Shaq's boss!"

For better or worse, great wealth brings great influence, and both Van Andel and DeVos exercise significant clout in Republican party politics. They became White House insiders during the tenure of President Gerald Ford, who originally represented the Grand Rapids district in the United States Congress. They also enjoyed access with both Reagan and Bush during their presidencies as well as to other leaders such as Senator Bob Dole and House Speaker Newt Gingrich.

But to DeVos and Van Andel, and to the second generation in both families, the first priority has always been Amway itself. They chose not to take the common route of building a big company, cashing out, and using the resulting fortune to move on to other things. To the contrary, Amway is the end game for them. It is not a stepping stone to some other goal, but is rather the thing itself which still commands their energy and attention.

The game plan seems clear: the company's formative period, with all its hazards and hard lessons, is behind. The kinks have been worked out of the system. The second generation of leadership is securely in place. Now the goal is to push the remarkable record of growth into the next century, until Amway has become one of the world's largest companies of any type, and to achieve all this by creating thousands of self-made business people among the ranks of its distributors.

As one member of the founding families said recently: "The pieces are all in place, and we expect an explosion of growth in the next ten years. Now we're just looking for 'a few good men' — and women!" Few observers doubt that they will find them.

3

Myths and Misconceptions

There is perhaps no company in America about which there is more *mis*information than Amway.

One reason is that virtually everyone in the country has heard something about Amway. Jay Leno makes jokes about it; everyone's brother-in-law has a story to tell about it; it's a can't-miss topic on those late night radio talk shows — just give people a chance to talk about Amway, and the switchboards light up. But for all of Amway's name recognition, the public awareness of exactly what the company really is and does remains remarkably thin.

Part of the blame for that belongs to Amway itself. For years, many Amway distributors were so secretive about their business that they created the impression they had something to hide. As the reputation of Amway as a solid, mainstream company grows, the practice of being secretive is falling away.

Another reason for the lack of public understanding of Amway is that its corporate strategy has always been *not* to advertise. This is a rather daring approach, given the ad-intensive nature of the personal products industry. Proctor and Gamble, for example, spent over $8.3 *billion* — a quarter of its total revenue — on marketing and TV advertising in 1995. The Amway corporate strategy is to spend a similar percentage of its revenue on marketing as Proctor and Gamble does, but Amway sends the money to its distributors rather than to TV networks and ad agencies.

In fact, all those millions of dollars that seem to be lining the pockets of successful Amway distributors are the very same dollars that are *not* being spent on national television advertising. But in the America of the 1990s, nothing seems to be real, and certainly not important, unless it's on television. So if Amway is not shouting its slogans in million-dollar sports TV spots, how important can the company be? At least, that's the type of question the popular mind asks.

A third reason Amway is misunderstood is simply that it is changing so fast. What was true about it ten years ago may no longer be true today. This is a company that is constantly reinventing itself, at a speed much faster than the average corporation, because its network of ordinary people puts it in touch with Joe Citizen every day. As a result, Amway responds to changes in public trends and consumer patterns more quickly than do the big-name corporate giants like General Motors, IBM, and Mitsubishi.

So lots of people know *about* Amway, but most don't know much, and much of what they do know is wrong. There is a kind of Amway mythology out there. Millions of people who first heard about Amway twenty years ago assumed it was a fad of some sort and would soon vanish like the hula hoop and eight-track tapes. They are startled to learn that not only is it still around, but it is also growing faster than ever and is now *five times* larger than it was when it first created headlines and jokes at cocktail parties in the early 1980s.

One thing is clear: this Amway thing refuses to die. It has survived the embryonic period of working out the kinks in its system, has learned to capitalize on the energy and direction of an emerging high-tech marketplace, and is quietly becoming a major force in venues where it was once ignored or ridiculed. Increasingly, the same people who dismissed it as unimportant ten years ago are now trying to figure out what makes it tick and how to make it work for them.

To understand Amway, one must begin by understanding what it is *not*.

1. It is NOT a soap company.

Soap? You want soap? Amway stills sell soap; but now it makes and markets four hundred products and provides service tie-ins like MCI long-distance telephone as well as a shoppers' catalog about as thick as the Manhattan phone book that handles thousands of name-brand items. No, it's no longer a soap company. Amway is "just a soap company" like Ross Perot is "just a computer salesman."

2. It is NOT a red-white-and-blue patriotic deal.

Would it surprise you to know that there is more Amway business being done *outside* America than *inside*? In Japan alone, it is now among the top five U.S.-based companies, so big it has spun off a separate New York Stock Exchange corporation just to handle the Japanese action. In the 1970s, *Forbes* magazine described Amway as a company that succeeds "by wrapping itself in the American flag." That description no longer makes sense. Does anyone really believe hundreds of thousands of Japanese (or German or Brazilian) distributors stand around and sing "God Bless America" at Amway Japan rallies?

3. It is NOT a door-to-door business.

Door-to-door sales and recruiting ended in the 1960s. The Amway concept could now be characterized as *interactive distribution,* and the shift is more than merely a name change. The whole idea of knocking on a stranger's door and trying to sell Amway products like Girl Scout cookies is so absurd, even Amway people laugh at it. Ask yourself this question: Have I personally *ever* had a stranger ring my doorbell and try to sell me some Amway soap? Not likely. It just isn't done door-to-door style and hasn't been for many years.

So if Amway no longer fits those old myths and stereotypes, what is it and how does it work?

In the vocabulary of Amway, a presentation of what it is and how it works is called the *plan.* Explaining the details is called *showing the plan,* and going through this routine is the quintessential behavior of the distributor who seeks to bring other people into his/her business network. Sometimes distributors refer to showing the plan as *drawing the circles* because the marketing system is explained by use of a diagram in which circles represent people.

When career Amway distributors show the plan, they spend the better part of an evening doing the job and may spend literally a lifetime refining their skill at it. As a marketing concept, for sheer intellectual exercise, the Amway plan is a complex and intriguing system, and it cannot be adequately explained in a few pages of print. But there is some Amway vocabulary that outsiders can learn, which helps them at least to understand the personal anecdotes distributors tell.

The following is a quick, simple glossary of Amway

jargon which will help translate some of the stories told in this book:

Interactive Distribution

This means that Amway delivers its products from the factory to the consumer by means of the direct interaction between a distributor and his/her customers. Traditional companies sell their products to retail stores, then spend big bucks on advertising to lure customers into those stores to buy the products. After the manufacturer makes its money, two other players must take out their chunk — the retail store and the advertiser. Instead, Amway says to its distributor: You can be both the store and the advertiser by selling, merchandising and building one's network person-to-person, and we will give you *both* chunks of the money. In a nutshell, that's why an Amway distributorship can be so lucrative.

Sponsoring

In addition to making money by selling products personally, Amway distributors can also make money — far *more* money, in fact — by recruiting other people to become distributors, which is called *sponsoring*. Thus, if Jack persuades Joe to become an Amway distributor, and Joe recruits Bill, Jack is paid a bonus based on the products and services sold by both Joe and Bill, and all the subsequent Bills, forevermore. The key to all this is that the bonus is not taken out of Joe and Bill's incomes — if it were, the baloney would eventually be sliced so thin that the whole system would collapse. Instead, Jack's bonus for sponsoring Joe is paid *by the home office* from its profits. So the myriad of bonuses can grow to include thousands of distributors, which gives the potential for huge incomes for those who build big networks.

Downline Leg

Those distributors Jack sponsors are called his *downline* distributors, and each line of them is referred to as a *leg*.

PV

The amount of retail sales is described by a formula which converts raw dollars into something called *PV* (for point value). Actually, this is just another way of talking about the total volume a distributor generates.

Direct Distributor

At a certain level of *PV*, a distributor reaches the status called *direct distributor*, which provides additional income and some extra perks. Reaching that level is the first major goal of new distributors and is referred to as *going direct*. The sponsor who helps one of his downline legs get to this level calls it *breaking a direct*.

Pin Awards

The Amway home office recognizes and rewards people on the basis of how many of their legs reach the level of direct. Many of the more significant payoffs in Amway are attached to these levels, along with a lapel pin, which is like the stripes on an officer's uniform in the Army. Breaking three direct legs earns an Emerald Pin; breaking six makes one a Diamond; twelve, a Double Diamond, and so on. The highest pin award is called Crown Ambassador.

Admittedly, this is a brief and incomplete introduction to Amway vocabulary, but it at least will allow you to get by. Like a traveler in a foreign country with a Berlitz phrase book, you now know just enough to understand what the natives are saying.

4

A Customized Business

Much of the genius of the Amway corporate operation is that it respects the ability of distributors to bring their own individual styles and strengths to the business. Amway avoids the temptation to overmanage from the top down. It allows for creative retooling by leaders in the field, who tailor the specific operation of their own distributorships to suit their own tastes.

This basic strength of the Amway concept flows naturally from its historic insistence that all distributors own their own businesses. They are not employees of Amway, not even commissioned salespersons. Each owns a private business, and within a few basic parameters set by the corporation is free to build that business in the way that works best then and there.

The basic parameters are important, and the company enforces them energetically: the quality and price of the products themselves; the marketing plan, with its various levels of pay and bonuses; the code of ethics, including such things as misrepresentation and tampering with someone else's distributor network. In these larger issues, Amway is Amway, wherever it is found, and it is practiced uniformly around the world.

But beyond that, any distributor can devise whatever *system* he chooses. The outcome is that the Amway business, after forty years of existence, operates in many varied forms. The basic elements are always the same, but the way it looks and feels at ground level may be very different from one distributorship to another.

An example: one distributor may emphasize a method of randomly soliciting prospects by use of telephone automatic-dialing equipment or by placing some version of help-wanted ads in local newspapers. But another distributor in the same city might instead feel that prospects are better solicited only from one's personal circle of friends, relatives, and neighbors. Which method is superior? There may be no sure answer. It could be argued that either method works equally as well as the other. The important point is that Amway Corporation encourages individual distributors to follow their line of sponsorship and to do what comes most naturally or works best in a particular time and place.

Over a period of years, Amway has established an overall corporate *strategy* but leaves the day-to-day *tactics* to the troops on the front lines. Amway Corporation is unusual in this way. In most national merchandising companies, the home office insists on a hard-and-fast conformity to a lock-step corporate model. Amway's flexibility has produced a global business and great resilience and adaptability.

The history of multilevel businesses is littered with the

corpses of new companies that have sprung up and flourished for a few years. These companies often compare themselves to Amway and recruit new distributors by pointing to their steep growth curves in those early years. Then, almost inevitably, they falter, collapse, and disappear.

Amway, on the other hand, is exceptionally resilient. Its ability to thrive through economic and sociopolitical ups and downs is virtually unprecedented in the history of multilevel companies. While similar companies have come and gone, Amway has shown a remarkable staying power. A major reason is that it constantly reshapes itself in the hands of any given distributor to the particular strengths and temperament of that distributor. Then, further, it gives that distributor the freedom to teach his uniquely crafted *system* to others, and entire subcultures that share that particular way of doing things develop within the Amway network.

In a sense, there are many Amways. One corporation, one product line, one code of ethics, one ingeniously devised marketing plan — but under that huge global canopy, many different clusters, each with its own personality.

In such a model, distributors in a particular cluster learn from their sponsors how to go about building their businesses. Obviously, all the businesses within a given line tend to use the same methods, to tell the same success stories, in effect to assume a similar personality. If Joe X shows the plan using an orange-colored marker, the person who first saw the plan in orange markers is likely to use an orange marker himself and so on and so on. Orange markers become part of that distributor's perception of "the way it's done."

An orange marker has nothing whatever to do with Amway itself, but to the prospect or new distributor, it may seem to be an inherent part of it. Clearly, some of the elements of a particular group's business personality are not so trivial as the color of the marker one uses! Some are so important that they define Amway itself, at least to the prospect.

An example: In a certain group in a Southern city — let's say Orlando — the leader of the group is a housewife, late middle-aged, who was attracted to Amway because it gave her an opportunity to earn a couple hundred dollars extra each month by selling Amway products to a few of her neighbors in her spare time. This was a perfect match to what she was seeking in a direct-sales business: by investing a small amount of time, she could earn a small income, mostly from selling household or personal care products to her friends. It gives her an opportunity to socialize, fills some of the empty hours created when her children grew up and left home, and provides a few dollars of spending money. It works for her. It meets her needs. It is her version of Amway, and it is a good one — for her.

Mrs. Orlando occasionally shares her good fortune with a friend by explaining her Amway business. When they show interest, she sponsors them. Over the years, her network grows into a sizeable group of such women, all with similar needs and a similar approach to Amway.

People who know Mrs. Orlando — relatives and friends who hear her discuss her business — think they know what Amway is and how it works. They are only partially right.

The personality of Mrs. Orlando's Amway group differs sharply from another group across the state. Let's call it Clearwater. In that town, a young couple, he an accountant, she a public school teacher, have grown disenchanted with their jobs and want a mid-life career change. They are energetic and ambitious but aren't inclined to do something extreme, such as going back to law school or medical school or training for an entirely new profession. They have little money to invest in a business of their own, but they have lots of time and energy and, most of all, lots of dreams of a brighter future for their family. They come into Amway looking for a new career that can be built with "sweat equity." They are willing to work hard for several years if their effort will produce a better life.

Mr. and Mrs. Clearwater do *not* want to sell a little toothpaste over coffee-table conversations a couple of mornings a month; they want a challenge that will absorb and reward an all-out commitment. So they build their business that way, and it works. They sponsor new people by offering the same dream that attracted them. They give a five-evening-per-week effort, and they challenge people in their group to do the same. They eat, sleep, and breathe Amway, just as the local clothing store owner or lawyer would his business. It rewards them lavishly.

To Mrs. Orlando, Amway means one thing; to Mr. and Mrs. Clearwater, it means something quite different. The personalities of their groups are so dissimilar that they hardly seem to be in the same business. Obviously, the contrasts in their goals, their expectations, and what they seek *from* their business will produce many other differences in the way they go about it.

Mrs. Orlando has a fairly static set of retail customers. She doesn't particularly want to add customers, much less to sponsor people, because that would mean opening her circle to an influx of strangers, which would miss the whole point. What she is doing is comfortable to her; she has no need of motivation or encouragement because her entire Amway operation comes naturally to her, and she has little desire for it to grow larger. For her, attending a motivational rally once a month to recharge her emotional batteries would be a waste of time. Nor would she wish to hear tapes or read books that offer training or inspiration through telling other Amway success stories. Nor would she be especially attracted by a promotional contest that might send her to Honolulu; she went once and didn't like it, and besides, her husband hates the sun.

Mr. and Mrs. Clearwater, on the other hand, feed off the inspiration and modeling contained in tapes and books. They enjoy going to rallies or weekend seminars because at such meetings they can see and hear what others are doing and what's working, which always encourages and motivates them. The constant interaction with other distributors is fun to them; it reminds them that there is another world beyond the one they are seeking to escape. And they love Honolulu!

So the Clearwater's Amway experience is filled with these elements, though they are entirely missing from the Amway experience of Mrs. Orlando. Obviously, the contrast in their two approaches to the business is more fundamental than orange markers versus black markers.

If, by chance, Mr. and Mrs. Clearwater had been initially introduced to Amway by someone in Mrs. Orlando's group, they would likely have (a) rejected it immediately, judging it to be irrelevant to their needs; or (b) signed up but quickly grown frustrated and dropped out, deciding it was a nice bunch of sweet little ladies that lacked the scope and power to deliver to them their dreams.

On the other hand, Mrs. Orlando would have been equally ill-served by the Clearwater approach. If someone from *that* group had first explained Amway to her, she would have either (a) been scared to death by its potential for upsetting her happy life; or (b) signed up but dropped out because she felt constant pressure to go to seminars and rallies, buy books and tapes, and sponsor new distributors.

In both cases, the mismatched prospects would have decided Amway was not for them — and would have been only half right! In fact, the Clearwater approach to Amway is right for the Clearwaters, and the Orlando version is perfect for Mrs. Orlando. This example, though obviously overdrawn, illustrates how differently the various groups of Amway distributors can explain, teach, and operationalize the same marketing plan.

Amway Corporation itself scrupulously avoids endorsing with a broad brush any and all of the contrasting approaches to the business. To the corporate officers in Michigan, it is an article of faith that there is no right or wrong way, that the business is designed to fit a variety of goals and levels of involvement, and that it can be as small or as large a part of the distributor's life as she or he desires.

Still, the corporation's neutrality notwithstanding, there is a kind of Darwinian scorekeeping which goes on, a survival of the fittest, in which it is clear that certain philosophies and approaches *do* in fact work better than others. Over the years, the numbers do not lie. Certain ways of building an Amway business persist and thrive at a higher rate than others. Distributors doing the business according to those models grow faster, make more money, and survive more adversity, and their numbers as a percentage of the overall Amway community dramatically increase. They must be doing something right.

The marketplace, as always, offers the ultimate test. Success itself, sustained over many years, becomes the ultimate judge of whether a particular *system* for doing Amway is a superior one.

If one analyzes the Amway business in this fashion, the telltale record of sustained success leads inevitably to Charlotte, North Carolina, and an unusual couple of transplanted New Yorkers named Dexter and Birdie Yager.

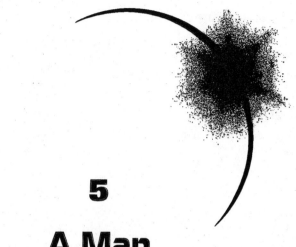

5

A Man
Named Dexter

Appearances are often deceiving. No bit of wisdom is more commonly understood than this. "Never judge a book by its cover," the saying goes.

And it is true. It is more true, perhaps, of people than of anything else. When sizing up any individual, be aware that the package can often be misleading. One modern historian illustrates this point by pointing to Winston Churchill, a man whom most regard to be one of the greatest leaders of this century. He was a gigantic figure who changed the course of human history. But virtually all his qualities of greatness were invisible at first appearance, states historian Norman Rose, who reminds us that Churchill was short, fat, gruff, constantly smoking a smelly cigar, opinionated, and often so preoccupied with whatever was going on inside his head that he appeared to be impolite and disinterested in people around him. In short, he didn't make a great first impression.

But there was much more to Winston Churchill than the first impression. In fact, says Rose, with Churchill you learned everything about him you didn't like the first time you saw him and then spent the rest of your life learning the things about him that made him great.

To a considerable degree, that is the way people experience Dexter Yager. He is a man very easy to underestimate. All the things one sees at first meeting send the signal that this is an ordinary man; it is later that the qualities of greatness emerge and dominate. At first impression, in fact, he shares much of Churchill's misleading exterior: He is short, rounded, and given to the occasional cigar (the latter two more evident in his past); he is strongly committed to opinions, which are stated in an emphatic and often challenging manner. He favors slacks and T-shirts rather than the businessman's uniform coat and tie. He makes no attempt to disguise his lack of a college background. It would be easy to meet Dexter Yager and write him off as an ordinary Southern good ol' boy.

Oh no. Never judge a book by its cover, especially this one. If it is true that Churchill showed people at first meeting a misleading exterior, and then they spent a lifetime admiring all the rest of him, the same can be said of Dexter Yager.

In almost four decades of Amway history, the attempt to find the perfect way of doing the business has been something of a Holy Grail. The number of individuals who have sought to create their own personalized approach to the Amway operation would be difficult to estimate, but surely it has been tens of thousands of them. Amway has a built-in selection factor that is always at work: It selectively attracts people who are ambitious and self-confident; then it rewards those within that group who are doggedly persistent. It is an entrepreneurial version of Darwin's principle of survival of the fittest. The lazy and timid never sign up, and if they do, they never last. The result is to produce a large population of assertive, sometimes aggressive, and self-assured men and women who are always looking for better and better ways to do the Amway business.

In this long history, many successful distributors have created their own *systems* of building profitable businesses, but no one has done it better than Dexter Yager. This makes little sense if one examines the usual factors for predicting who might build a vast business empire. Yager doesn't match up to many of the typical criteria:

- College degree: none

- Family background in finance: none

- Capital assets at the start of the business: none

- Training to be a certified public accountant or to receive a master's in business administration: none

- Memberships in country clubs, Rotary, and so on: none

- Previous business ownership: none

Yet this fifty-six-year-old businessman leads a worldwide organization that is generally regarded to be the largest and most profitable in Amway's global distributor force, although the insistence of Amway Corporation on the privacy of distributor incomes prevents anyone from awarding such a distinction officially. One thing is sure: hundreds of Diamonds and hundreds of thousands of distributors have looked to him for leadership over the past quarter-century, and few dispute that his *system* — his approach to the business — has created more success for more people over a longer period of time than any other.

Yager now lives in Florida, though his Amway business originally flourished in Charlotte, North Carolina, in his adopted region of the Deep South. His career began, however, in a place far removed, geographically and culturally, from the suburban North Carolina, where he would build his base and perfect his system. He is a native of a tough blue-collar area of upstate New York; he was born in Fulton and experienced his childhood and adolescence, and began his Amway business, in the hardscrabble town named Rome.

Yager was born in 1939 into a working-class family that was fairly typical of the region in those years, Irish-English descent on his mother's side, German-Scottish on his father's side. The family name Yager meant "get your gun and go" in German, he was told, and Dexter was his mother's maiden name. He was the second oldest of five children.

The Yagers were Protestants in a largely Catholic region, and religion was always an important part of their lives. They worshiped at both Methodist and Baptist churches at various times, and religious identity was never much of an issue to them, except that being non-Catholic gave them a sense of being in the minority. They were politically conservative and considered themselves to be Republicans, although party labels were never a major concern, either. Birdie's family supported Democratic president Harry Truman in his famous comeback election in 1948, but the Yagers were always strong Republicans who cared more about individual candidates and issues than about party alignment.

Generally, the Yager family style was not to care much about labels of any kind but to care deeply about basic conservative values. Theirs was a traditional American conservatism of the old-fashioned kind that reached powerfully into every part of young Dexter's life. The values were simple and nonnegotiable: A man works hard; he never asks for a handout; he can be trusted; his word is his bond; a man shows respect to the basic institutions of society — the church, the government, the military; a man takes responsibility for those who depend on him, especially his family and his friends; a man does his duty — he serves his country if he is called, pays his debts, and keeps his commitments; a man stands on his own two feet; he makes his own way; and he will pay almost any price to be free.

Dexter Yager was part of that in-between generation, born too late to be considered baby boomers, but not old enough to have experienced World War II, which was the defining experience of the generation slightly older. His clearest memory of the war was his father's hatred of Hitler and accompanying frustration at not being allowed to join the Army to fight against the Nazis. "Dad really hated Hitler, probably even more so because his background was German. As soon as the war started, even though he had children, Dad went to the recruiting office but couldn't pass the physical because he had a hernia. He tried to sign up in all three branches, but they wouldn't take him because of that hernia. Even though he shouldn't have, I think he felt just a bit ashamed that he wasn't over there fighting for his country."

* * * * *

The fierce instincts of the entrepreneur surfaced in Dex Yager's personality early. Though his family trade was plumbing, the plumbers in his background took pride in being businessmen-plumbers, rather than working for a safe wage in another man's operation. Royal J. Yager, Dexter's grandfather, owned his own plumbing shop, as did his uncle and others in the family. "From the time I was

51

a little boy," he recalls, "I had it hammered into me that owning your own business and working for yourself was the way to go. In fact my mother always told me that being a Yager means you don't work for someone else!"

Dexter's father was emphatically in agreement with that family principle, even though he joined the local chapter of the plumbers union at one point in his life, a decision that was prompted by necessity and that apparently cut painfully against the grain for the independent-minded elder Yager. He eventually became treasurer of the local chapter, but he always resented the fact that he had been forced to join the union to get work.

Apart from that single concession to organized labor, the family tradition tilted heavily toward risk-taking and personal initiative. Dexter learned to love the idea of living by his skills and wits in the rough-and-tumble atmosphere of the free marketplace. It didn't take long for his entrepreneurial flair to express itself in the tangible form of a neighborhood Kool-Aid punch stand.

The Yager family lived in a large housing development. When young Dexter was a sixth grader, he watched as construction began on a large apartment complex next door. The weather was hot; scores of laborers were on the job site; and Dex saw an opportunity. He mixed up a batch of sugary Kool-Aid, hustled over to the construction site, and sold a few cups of it. *Not bad but not terrific either,* Dex thought, and the light turned on when one of his customers, reluctantly paying for a cup of Kool-Aid, told him, "We don't like Kool-Aid, son; what we want is pop."

Gotcha. Dexter folded down the Kool-Aid stand, scooped up his available cash, ran to the nearest grocery store, bought a couple of six-packs of soft drinks, ran home, grabbed a metal trash can, filled it with ice cubes from his mother's refrigerator, went back to the construction site, and promptly sold out. From that point, the volume escalated rapidly. Within a few days, Dex was set up semi-permanently in a garage on the edge of the work site with a big washbucket. Eventually, he had the ice man delivering ice every morning and a soda company delivering cases of soft drinks, and every day he did business with dozens of thirsty construction workers. *If it's pop they want, then I'm in the pop business,* Yager figured. An entrepreneur was born.

He did other jobs as well through those childhood years. He ran a paper route, mowed lawns in the summer, and shoveled driveways in the winter; there was no odd job he would not do. He was stimulated by the work itself, the chance to do something someone else needed, and the reward of being paid for getting it done. And school? "I wasn't crazy about school. I enjoyed being around the other kids, but basically school was boring to me. One year I tried to be on the honor roll, and I made the honor roll, but there were no perks that went with it, so I wasn't interested anymore. In elementary school, I was pretty good at skipping class; then it got more and more boring, and by the time we got to junior high, I was a *pro* at skipping class!"

It was to be that way for Yager throughout high school: work was challenging and school was not, so he gravitated more and more toward the world of business. By the time he was sixteen years old, school was merely something to endure until afternoons, weekends, or summertime, when he could get a real job. He was always good at math and was even accused of cheating at math on one occasion because he was able to do the computations in his head but couldn't show the teacher the mathematical steps on paper. "When you are a kid, and you're making money all the time, you're counting it up in your head, on your paper route or whatever. You're always computing whether you're broke, or how much you're making. You normally can learn to do a lot of math in your head before you ever get to those classes. That's the way I was. I could get to the answer, but I couldn't always explain to the teacher how I got there."

He hated history. He hated English. He was restless in the way of all bright students who are unchallenged, who fail to see the connection between schoolwork and the rest of life. He performed well in the classroom when he chose to, which was rare, and he looked for things to do that interested him, like running the film projector for his teachers, which got him out of class. He never had significant disciplinary problems but was frequently in the doghouse for skipping class. He respected his teachers and gave them no trouble, but they were frustrated by what they considered the loss of his potential because he tested extremely high on their IQ tests, yet he had little interest in academic life. Basically, he did his time. He respected his parents' desire for him to graduate, so he stayed in school, but what drew him was never the quiet, slow life of the classroom, but the action and competition of doing business in the real world.

Fish gotta swim; birds gotta fly; Dex Yager gotta do business. It was like a law of nature. And as surely as God gave gills to the fish and wings to the birds, God gave Yager an instinct for entrepreneurial leadership that made it virtually inevitable, even from his youngest days, that he would create something of significance in the world of business. But that would come later. First, there would be some growing up to do, some lessons to learn, and a girl named Birdie.

6

Birdie

Dexter Yager and Birdie Narehood were classic examples of teenage sweethearts whose dreams and instincts were so compatible that they never outgrew one another.

Birdie was the baby girl in a family of sixteen children. Her father worked in the mill and had a small farm. Rome, New York, was not a large town, and Dexter and Birdie barely remember meeting one another; they were always just there, part of the same social group even before junior high school. She was a few months younger than Dex and one year behind him in school.

In a sixteen-child family like the Narehoods where there is pride and self-respect, everyone works hard simply to survive, and Birdie developed an appetite for hard work and achievement. In addition to running a large household, Birdie's mother found ways to supplement the family income, doing the odd wallpapering job, cleaning offices. She was a relentless bargain shopper, buying clothes for her children at rummage sales and Salvation Army stores. She was not a passive woman, and she did not raise a passive daughter.

Dexter and Birdie were two kids growing up together in the same small town, hanging out with different crowds. Her parents knew his parents, no big deal. But at some point, Dex began to notice Birdie, really *notice* her: "During the summertime, we would all go to a place called Sylvan Beach, about twenty-five miles away, where they had a beach and a ferris wheel and rides and stuff. They had bingo there and dance bands for the parents, and the kids played on the beach. When I was about fifteen, some of us were horsing around on the beach. One particular day, I remember Birdie had something and I was trying to take it away from her, and suddenly I remember seeing her very differently, you know? It was just a moment. I wasn't dating her or anyone else at the time; we were just kids horsing around on the beach, but there was this spark that day. She probably doesn't remember it, but something clicked for me."

Dex did nothing about it right away. No need — he saw Birdie at school, at the skating rink, around town. She was always in his general environment. Eventually, though, the time came for him to follow up in a more purposeful way.

It was early in his senior year at high school that Dex pushed the relationship up a notch: "I remember distinctly. It was a summer day before my senior year. A buddy and I were driving around in his car, and we saw Birdie and one of her girlfriends coming toward us. She was driving her dad's Oldsmobile, and she waved at us; she had long brunette hair waving in the wind, and I looked over at my buddy, and I said 'Hey, look at that Birdie. I'm going to start dating her.' And he just said, 'Yeah, sure.' But I did. I saw her a little later, sitting on the front porch of her friend Kate Kimpton's house, on one of those porch swings. And I just pulled over and started talking and asked her out.

"We dated a few times, and then she went to New York City to visit her sister for a couple of weeks, and I was surprised at how much I missed her. I got a postcard from her with 'I miss you' and stuff like that, and that really lit me up. So when she got home, all of a sudden, it was every day, all the time. It wasn't long until all we wanted to do was graduate from high school so we could get married."

And that's what they did, at the age of seventeen, both finishing high school as they had promised their parents. There was never any thought of college. They had dreams: they wanted a home, they wanted a family, they wanted to build a life together, and they were prepared to work hard to fulfill their desires. It was time to go to work; no more Kool-Aid stands. Dexter Yager had a wife, it wouldn't be long before babies would be on the way, and it was time for some serious income.

Dex had worked throughout high school at Simpkins Clothing Store, sweeping floors, keeping the shelves stocked, and occasionally subbing for a salesman when someone missed work. During the summers, he had worked a second job as a laborer on various construction crews in the area. He grasped quickly the greater income potential of sales commissions over hourly wages but lacked confidence in his ability to make a living at sales, so he looked for a job working with his hands.

With the ink barely dry on both his high school diploma and his marriage certificate, Yager applied for a job at Sears. The local Sears store was in a strip mall in Rome, and Yager saw a newspaper ad describing an opening for an auto mechanic in the garage. It was a place to start. When he arrived to interview for the job, he was told it had already been filled, so he turned to walk out the door. The assistant manager stopped him: "Wait a minute. We just had an opening for a salesman in the hardware department. Would you be interested in that?"

"No, sir," Yager responded without hesitation. "I'm no good at sales."

"That's OK," the manager said. "Take the job anyway, and you can just do sales as you feel more comfortable with it."

And with that the deal was made. Yager went to work in the Sears hardware department, still scared that he wouldn't be able to sell anything, and soon became a first-rate salesman. The assistant manager spotted his natural ability, taught him all he knew, gave him confidence, and took pleasure in watching his young protégé grow. Within a year, the assistant manager was promoted, and Yager was virtually running the department.

But families of two have a way of becoming families of three, or in the Yagers' case, four. In less than a year-and-a-half, Birdie gave birth to twin boys, Dexter Jr. and Doyle, and Daddy felt the need for more income than the Sears job could provide.

7

Beyond Sears

Yager had loved automobiles since he was a child. He loved to drive them, polish them up, work under the hood — anything that had to do with cars, he enjoyed doing it. Sociologists are quick to point out that the entire post-World War II generation had a love affair with the automobile, and in that respect, Yager was certainly a child of his generation.

"My dad owned a Plymouth station wagon, and I was always going out washing it, waxing it. I would buy little gadgets and put them on Dad's cars just like they were my own." Dex bought his first car when he was only fifteen years old, he recalls, "but my dad made me take it back until I was old enough for a driver's license." His next "first car" was a '47 Dodge, already an old heap when he bought it from a buddy. He scraped all the paint off with a razor blade, sanded it down, then traded it in for a '49 Dodge coupe before he even got it repainted.

Yager became a good mechanic. He and his buddies took turns working on each other's cars because they couldn't afford to pay someone to work on them and because they enjoyed doing it. It was pure recreation for them. "Cars were always a major, major dream to me. It was a lot more than transportation. I started loving cars before I can even remember."

It was inevitable that when car-crazy Yager began looking for a job, car salesman would be his occupation of choice. While still a teenager, he went to the local Chevrolet dealership in Rome and applied for a job as a salesman. The manager of the dealership turned him down on the spot, no reasons given. Dex persisted, telling him how much he loved cars and how much he knew about them. "It makes no difference," the Chevy dealer told him. "You'll never be a salesman. You just don't qualify." Then he gave Yager all the reasons he could never make it as a salesman. "First," Dex recalls, "I had a small speech impediment. I stuttered a little bit when I got nervous. He pointed that out and then told me all the other reasons I could never be a salesman. And I accepted it! I figured he must know what he was talking about, so I let him convince me."

That's how Yager ended up with a job at the local Sears store in the hardware department. He began with barely enough confidence to ring up items on the cash register, but things changed during the three years Yager worked at Sears. He showed himself that in fact he *could* sell, at least small-ticket items in a hardware department, and that when he got his mind off himself and began to focus on the customer, his stutter disappeared. And something else changed — he had two new little mouths to feed, twin boys.

Looking for ways to survive on his Sears income, Dex decided to trade his car for a pickup truck, on the basis that operating a truck would be less expensive. He stopped by the local Ford dealership and explained to the sales manager, a friend named Stan, that he was looking for a pickup. "A pickup truck? Why a pickup truck?" Stan asked incredulously, and Yager explained that his reasons were economic. Stan answered immediately, "You don't need a pickup truck. What you need is to come work for me as a salesman, and you won't have to drive a pickup truck."

"No can do," Yager replied. He told him about what the Chevy dealer had said years before about how he could never be a salesman. Stan wouldn't buy it: "Yeah, right, Dex, and in case you haven't noticed, that Chevy place isn't even open anymore! They didn't know their business, Dex! You come to work for me, and I'll train you, and I guarantee you'll make a great salesman."

"How can you be so sure?" Yager wanted to know.

"You know Billy June?" Stan asked.

"Sure, I sold him a lawn mower," said Dex.

"Right," Stan shot back. "You sold him a lawn mower, and you sold about half a dozen more of my salesmen lawn mowers. Nobody else down at Sears ever did that. You're a natural-born salesman, Dex, and if you can sell lawn mowers, you can sure sell Fords!"

He convinced Yager, who went home and told Birdie that he was going to work selling cars at the Ford dealership. The next day he went to see the manager at Sears and told him he intended to work out his two weeks' notice. His boss, obviously surprised, responded angrily, "You can't work out a two weeks' notice — you're through as of right now!"

So Yager was immediately unemployed. "I called Stan at the Ford place and asked him what was I supposed to do for the next two weeks, and he told me to come to work for him tomorrow morning, and that was that."

For the next three years, Yager sold new and used cars at Ed Maxwell Ford on the main highway going through town. He was guaranteed sixty dollars a week against his commissions, plus a company car. He was good at his job, and it served him well. The dealership owned a small house next to the car lot, which Dex and Birdie rented and fixed up as their new home. Dex worked from 8:00 in the morning until after midnight many nights, but still there was very little income left over at the end of the week. They were struggling, but they were young and in love, and they were making it.

In those three years, Yager created a reputation in Rome as a top-notch salesman. Other car lots tried to hire him away; the Cadillac dealership offered him a job. He was developing a name for himself.

None of that mattered, however, when Ed Maxwell, the owner of the business, died. No one knew what would happen, but Dex noticed that the men running the dealership began cutting the orders for new cars and sharply reducing inventory, and change was obviously coming. Yager heard rumors, saw various employees being laid off or repositioned in an apparent prelude to the sale of the business. A group of businessmen even offered to back him financially if he would buy out the Ford dealership. Suddenly Dex realized that no matter how well he performed as a salesman, his job was fundamentally insecure because the bottom line was that *it was not his business.*

Seeing the inescapable insecurity of his occupation (the dealership eventually closed), Yager decided to look for something else. Once again he resigned, betting that he could find something better. This time he stayed unemployed longer than just overnight; for almost a month he answered ads, weighed possibilities, and grew more and more restless.

Dex and Birdie had a growing family by this time. Sixteen months after the twins, a daughter April was born, followed quickly by Lisa. Then came Jeff, Leanne, and Steven. It was between child No. 3 and child No. 4 that Dex left his job at Ford, and Birdie had not worked outside the home after having children. But things suddenly were very tight financially, with Dex out of work, so Birdie decided to try to find work. She and Dex both applied for jobs at a local military base.

The unthinkable happened: Birdie was offered a job, and Dexter was rejected. He was mortified. "It was a real ego thing at that point. I failed the typing part of the job test, so I didn't have enough points, but Birdie did OK, so they hired her and not me. I felt like a real dunce. Like, here's my wife with little kids, having to go back to work as a keypunch operator, and I don't even have a job. I felt like some kinda leech bum. It was bad."

When a job opportunity finally came through, it was an offer to distribute products for the West End Brewery, a local company that sold Utica Club beer. Yager called on bars, restaurants, and grocery stores. He took orders for beer, went into stores and put up displays, that sort of thing. It wasn't glamorous or exciting work but, along with Birdie's paycheck, it paid the bills. Barely.

They bought a small house on an alley; it was eighty years old and needed lots of work. Times were tough. Both of them were working long hours, juggling schedules with various babysitters, meeting one another as they passed on their way to and from their respective jobs. Nobody was having much fun, and whatever dreams they had from the newlywed years were fading rapidly.

"Birdie hated her job, and she hated having to work and be away from the kids. She would come home from work about 11:30 or midnight, and about once a week, we would have an all-night argument because Birdie would want to quit. She would be fed up with the way they treated her on the job. And I would say, 'Birdie, we bought this house. We've got to make these payments!' One night I got so mad I literally rammed my fist through the bedroom wall. I guess I was just trying to make a point. I was standing in the middle of the bed, and I'm not a violent person, but that night I just smashed the wall."

It was that kind of life.

It changed in 1964.

Not immediately, of course. The path that took the Yagers from the West End Brewery to head up one of America's most powerful direct-sales organizations would not be traveled overnight. But as the old Chinese proverb puts it, "The journey of a thousand miles begins with a single step," and the Yagers made that single step on November 1, 1964.

8

Yager Sees
the Circles

On that memorable night, Dex returned home from
work to find a note on the kitchen table. Birdie was
nowhere to be seen. The note said: "Dex, Russ is coming to
talk to you tonight about Amway. Please listen. Love, Birdie.
P.S. I've gone to Mom's."

Dex was trapped. "I was ticked off. I'd been out selling
all day long, and I was tired. I didn't need some guy coming into my house at night, talking to me about some deal I
didn't care anything about in the first place." The "Russ" in
Birdie's note was Russ Bingham, a young millworker who
had recently been laid off from work and who was a distant relative of Dexter's.

The note had said, "Please listen." That was the worst

part. It meant Birdie was appealing to her husband as a gentleman to give this Russ a fair hearing and not just hustle him out the door. Dex knew he had been set up. Obviously, Birdie had figured if she had asked, Dex would have told her not to set up the appointment. So she didn't ask. She just made the appointment for Russ, then skipped out to her mom's house, leaving Dex with no way to cancel the appointment. "It was like, she knew she was going to be in trouble, so she got outta the house," Yager explains.

Not only that, but what Russ wanted to talk about was Amway. Yager had already been approached on it twice before and thought it was some kind of door-to-door selling thing, and he wasn't interested. The reason Birdie had conspired with Russ to arrange the meeting was simple: she was desperate to quit her job and stay home with her kids, and she thought maybe Amway might be her ticket out.

She was right. Despite his resistance ("I just sat there with my arms crossed and let him talk. I was so ticked off"), Dex Yager sat through Russ's stumbling, nervous presentation of the Amway plan and liked what he saw. "I saw the numbers. And I understood the numbers. It didn't matter whether I respected Russ or anything else; it didn't matter how good or bad a job he did showing the plan; I understood the numbers, and I said, 'Alright, what do I do next?'"

Just like that, Dexter and Birdie Yager became Amway distributors. They attacked the business as if their lives were at stake. That very night, as soon as Dex signed up, he took Russ to a friend's house, had Russ show *him* the plan, and took notes this time so he would know how to do it himself. The friend joined. The next day, he went to another meeting to see the presentation again. The day after that, he sponsored someone else, and the Yagers were off and running.

At the end of December, their second month in the business, Yager paid out sixteen bonus checks, which meant he and Birdie had at least sixteen distributors who had themselves done more than a hundred dollars each in sales that month. He showed the plan every night to almost everyone he knew. He even gave his parents a distributor kit as a Christmas gift. He showed the plan to every brother and sister, virtually every old high school friend, and seemingly everyone he had worked with at Sears, the Ford place, the brewery, and the military base.

The Yagers reached seventy-five hundred dollars in volume the second month, which made them Silver Directs, as they were called at that time, and earned them a trip to corporate headquarters in Ada, Michigan. They toured the company facilities, met Rich DeVos and Jay Van Andel, and heard the news that Amway Corporation nationwide had done a total of thirty-six million dollars in estimated retail sales that year. "I thought that was an amazing, gigantic corporation. Today Amway worldwide is over six billion. Funny how your perspective changes, isn't it?"

Yager was working virtually around the clock. In order to free up his evenings to show the Amway plan, he reworked his schedule of calling on West End Brewery accounts. Some larger stores opened as early as 6:30 A.M., so he arranged to call on them at that time to get an early start. He estimates that he worked sixty hours a week on the brewery job and still showed the plan seven nights a week. He was obsessive: "Every time I laid down to sleep, I thought about circles and people's names I could put in them."

When time came to make the trip to Michigan for his Silver Direct seminar in January of 1965, Yager went to his supervisors to request time off for the trip. No way, they said. Even though he had a vacation coming, they told him he couldn't take the time off — the brewery had scheduled the grand opening of a new building, and Dex had to be there.

He had a choice to make. "It didn't take me long to think about it," Yager says. "I had already decided Amway was my future, not that brewery, so I said 'OK. I quit.'" Ready or not, Dexter and Birdie Yager became full-time Amway distributors. "I was a naive person in a lot of ways. If I had been older and more intelligent, I would probably have said, 'Well, I don't need to go on that trip.' But I was young and thought I knew what I was doing."

As it turned out, he knew exactly what he was doing.

* * * * *

Almost immediately after becoming direct distributors themselves, the Yagers began to see others whom they had sponsored go direct. Their income grew correspondingly until it exceeded a thousand dollars a month, more than they had brought home from their two regular jobs combined.

But after an initial explosion of success in their new business, the Yagers settled into a comfortable routine that soon became a rut. It wasn't as bad as the rut they had been in before, but it was a rut nevertheless.

The problem, they later recognized, was that the driving motivation for doing the business originally had been to quit their jobs at the brewery and the military base — for Dex to be his own boss and for Birdie to stay home and raise their children. That was the extent of their dream. There was nothing else. They had too little acquaintance with the lifestyles of the rich and famous to know how to dream boldly. Their dream was to be free, and they had achieved that dream.

What inevitably happened was that their success gradually eroded until they were making barely enough from the Amway business to replace their earlier income — in other words, barely enough to get by. In some motivational version of the law of gravity, life seems always to work that way: One's performance drifts down to the level of one's dreams. For the Yagers, what that meant was that they were free but broke. No nine-to-five job to worry about, but no money left over each month to provide a better life, either.

They were in a slump, professionally and personally. Amway had in fact given them all they had asked of it, but the problem was that they had asked very little.

Yager remembers those days with horror: "We wanted to be free, and we got what we wanted, but after that we didn't reset any other goals. So for three years we were Directs, but Directs that were barely making it. I realized my business wasn't going where I wanted it to go, and I started to get discouraged. I started listening to all the losers around me who were saying maybe Amway wasn't all it was cracked up to be."

The truth is this: The Yagers almost allowed their dream to die. "I don't like to admit it, but I said, 'Well, I'm never going to give up Amway altogether, but maybe I need to go get a job and go back to work.' So I went to check out the job market and find out what kind of job I could get." Yager went to an employment agency, and they sent him to a company that was advertising for a salesman to put their product in stores. Dex dutifully showed up at the appointed time for his job interview.

The job paid eight thousand dollars a year, and the interview was a disaster. In retrospect, it was the best thing that could have happened to the Yagers. Dex took a series of tests and filled out various questionnaires, then sat down for his interview with the personnel manager. He asked Dex what kind of job he would eventually like to have. Yager, in his typical blunt honesty, replied, "Well, I'd like to have *your* job someday."

Not a good answer. The personnel manager was not amused. He lit into Yager: "First," he said with a glare, "my job is not open. Second, the job you're interviewing for is strictly a salesman; there is no opportunity for advancement whatsoever for you in this job. Third, we require sharp people with outstanding personalities who have some class, and you don't fit the role. So you don't get the job because you're not classy enough to handle our specialized clients."

End of interview.

Yager walked out, and by the time he got home, his head had cleared, and he knew he was no longer a candidate for that or any other job. "That night I had a board meeting with Birdie. I told her I was thankful this had happened because it was my wake-up call. I had been making excuses. I had quit believing in me and had lost my excitement. Somehow during those three years, I had been lulled to sleep. I said to Birdie, 'What I need is not a job; what I need is to get my dream back. We've got to realize that from now on, it's Amway or nothing; this is our best, and maybe our only, hope!'"

Things changed in Dexter's attitude that night, and his business changed along with it, dramatically and permanently. With a regenerated commitment, he began showing the plan every night again, and the magic returned. He got his dream back. Business boomed. Within six months, the Yager distributorship was among the largest in the entire Amway world. Dexter had made a few trips to Florida to draw the circles and stopped in a city in North Carolina which he eventually fell in love with. He and Birdie decided to move their business to the warmer climate of the Deep South and settled in Charlotte, North Carolina. The move didn't slow their business growth at all. They continued to build their base in Rome, New York, expanded some other legs in the South, and, within two years, they had gone beyond Diamond to the Double Diamond level.

What happened? "I learned a lesson. I learned that you have to spend as much time cultivating your dream as you spend cultivating your business. If you let the dream die, everything else dies with it. I learned that I will never ever go on without a dream that's bigger than wherever I am at that time. And I also learned that I need help to keep my dream alive. I need positive books and tapes. I need to be challenged and grow. I need to program my mind constantly with material that builds my dream. Once I learned that, our business was never the same."

Dexter and Birdie Yager had made contact with the world of ideas that is found in books — positive, motivational books that showed them that their dreams, although not quite dead, had been small and puny and that a grander, more exciting world was out there for them beyond Rome, New York, beyond anything they had ever known or even imagined.

9

Creating a System

In the aftermath of the frustrating three-year slump, as Yager's young Amway distributorship took on new life, he began to place heavy emphasis on several business principles that quickly emerged as the trademarks of his style. These principles still persist today as the foundation blocks on which the Yager *system* is built. So many other successful entrepreneurs — inside and outside Amway — embrace and preach these ideas in the 1990s that it is difficult to remember that they were innovative and even controversial, at least to the degree that Yager espoused them, over thirty years ago. Although he makes no claim to inventing the concepts themselves, most Amway watchers agree that Yager was truly a pioneer in the extent to which he built them into his system as indispensable core elements.

These few principles he regarded as being almost as important as the marketing plan itself:

1. Dream building

2. Working in depth

3. Using tools to build attitudes

4. Mass meetings

Dream Building

Yager argues that the fuel that drives great individual effort is largely emotional — rather than mental or logical. And the most powerful human emotions are positive ones, not negative ones. So the starting place for building a new business must always be the act of igniting one's personal dreams. The bigger and more ambitious the dream, the better.

To secure a prospect's or distributor's commitment to this new Amway business, then, the primary effort should be spent not only in presenting a logical, intellectual business plan with all the facts and figures, but also in awakening the person's dormant desires and hungers. Once people have an active dream, Yager reasons, they will find the energy to pursue a business which can make the dream a reality.

Yager's sense that building one's dream is the most important element of success in a business such as Amway is probably the single most conspicuous aspect of his system. Several facts support this conclusion. Yager wrote a book in 1978, still in circulation today with sales beyond the one million mark, titled *Don't Let Anyone Steal Your Dream;* he and his Diamonds conduct annual business conferences called Dream Weekends; and the magazine published by his company is called *Dreambuilders.*

Obviously, Yager didn't spin this concept out of thin air. The importance of dreams has long been part of the rhetoric of salesmanship, and many writers and speakers before Yager had discussed it, including Amway president Rich DeVos, who had already gained a national reputation as a speaker on such themes long before Yager joined the Amway forces. The difference was in the priority which Yager assigned it. He recognized the risk that such constant talk of dreams might keep some observers from treating his new business seriously. There was always the possibility that his emphasis on the emotion of the business would draw criticism that there was little substance to it, that the whole business was merely hype and emotion.

But Yager accepted both the risks and the criticism. He avoided the trap of trying to legitimize Amway by accentuating its technical aspects. "I've never tried to make this business seem more complicated than it really is," he says. "In the early days, when no one had heard of Amway, one of our challenges was getting people to take us seriously as a serious business with serious potential. There was a fear that if we talked too much about the dreams, people would lose sight of the fact that we had great products and a solid company. But I have always felt that the dreams are what make people do this business, and I began to realize after the first few years that dreams are what we should always be talking about."

Working in Depth

When a beginning Amway distributor sponsors new people, and *they* in turn sponsor new people of their own, a basic question arises: How does one spend time more effectively? Is it more productive to continue personally sponsoring new distributors (creating *width* in the organization) or to help *those downline* sponsor new people (creating *depth*)?

Obviously, the best answer is to do both. A cardinal rule is that no distributor, no matter how successful or large his organization, ever quits personally sponsoring. But it is also true that there is a responsibility to help those people in his downline succeed by helping them build their own organizations. For a growing business, the question is one of balance and priority. There isn't enough time to do everything.

In the early years of his Amway career, Dexter Yager began to realize that the security and permanence of a large distributorship lay in its depth rather than its width. At that time, this view of the business was little understood, and the conventional wisdom was to emphasize heavily the need for frontline sponsoring.

Several factors discouraged a distributor from working in depth. First, the marketing plan itself made personal sponsoring extremely profitable. For a distributor's group to be very wide and shallow — that is, for most distributors to be personally sponsored by the leader — generates the highest levels of immediate income. Second, the Amway Corporation's *system* of recognizing achievement was based almost entirely on width. In awarding pins for various levels of success — Ruby, Pearl, Emerald, Diamond, and so on — the payoffs honored width almost totally to the exclusion of depth. Third, the philosophy of the business was that new direct distributors were expected to work on their own, to break off from a close working relationship with their sponsors and instead have a direct (hence the name) relationship with the corporation itself. The result was that many distributors who had enjoyed the nurture and guidance of their sponsors until they reached the direct level, suddenly found themselves nudged out of the nest and told to look directly to the corporation for leadership. For some distributors, like Yager himself, who had strong individual leadership skills, this *system* worked fine. But for many others, perhaps most others, the loss of upline leadership close to home was sorely missed, and often their growth stalled out at the direct level.

This approach was an intelligent and necessary one in the early development of Amway. It gave the corporation in Michigan an opportunity to monitor and influence closely the emerging shape of the business nationwide. In fact, it is no overstatement to say that this corporate emphasis was partially responsible for Amway's ability to develop into a multibillion-dollar enterprise while maintaining a tight and coherent core structure.

But Yager's instinct was that as Amway matured and grew, the ability of the corporation itself to provide nurture and motivation in a meaningful way for a growing army of distributors would diminish. For an individual distributorship to become a vast nationwide enterprise, resilient enough to survive the ups and downs of life over many decades, that distributorship must be very deep as well as very wide.

Again, as in the emphasis on dream building, Yager's breakthrough in this area was one of priority. He didn't invent the concept of working in depth or helping one's downline to grow, but he emphasized it far more than anyone before him. He virtually made it into a science. Ultimately, he would measure his own success and that of his colleagues, not by how many distributors were in his business, not even by how many directs, but by how many Diamonds!

Yager also grasped how much people need the richness of close personal relationships. He understood the value of mentors long before the concept became an organizational cliché. He became a father figure to many people who worked in depth and taught them how to invest likewise in other peoples' lives.

Using Tools to Build Attitudes

A basic premise of entrepreneurial life is that the entrepreneur's success depends on his or her attitude. Building one's own business is tough work. There are so many discouragements, so few guarantees, such a need to believe in future rewards before they are visible, that an upbeat and resilient mind-set is critically important.

Few people come naturally to the positive attitudes and never-say-die spirit they need to build a direct-sales business from the ground up. Even if by nature some people might tend to be upbeat and optimistic, the constant negative messages of a pessimistic culture are enough to drain their morale.

The solution is to combat all those negative messages with positive ones, delivered in the form of positive-thinking books, cassette tapes (once records or reel-to-reel tapes), and interaction with other distributors at mass meetings, sometimes with the emphasis on *mass* — huge crowds coming together to remind each other that good things can happen to people who work hard enough.

These business support materials, when used to build positive attitudes and openly share business techniques and principles, are as essential to an entrepreneur as hammer and saw are to a carpenter, Yager contends, and hence he calls them the "tools" with which one's business is built. And although he certainly didn't invent the idea that such tools are important, Dexter Yager clearly was the first to put tools at the heart of his Amway operation.

Almost from the beginning of Amway Corporation in 1959, its cofounders understood that distributors would benefit from an occasional infusion of positive ideas. Rich DeVos is a powerful public speaker, and he uses his ability with great effect. Even as a young man, he had the power to electrify crowds with his oratory, and one of his speeches, a patriotic message titled "Selling America," was recorded on a long-playing record — the best available technology of the time.

DeVos and his partner Jay Van Andel had earlier discovered the power of the written word to build their self-confidence and motivation. In addition to the classic Norman Vincent Peale work, *The Power of Positive Thinking,* they read books such as *Think and Grow Rich,* the story of Chicago insurance tycoon W. Clement Stone, and a short parable called *Acres of Diamonds* by Russell Conwell, and they recommended these books to their growing Amway network. There were only a handful of such books at that time.

As old-fashioned vinyl records and reel-to-reel tapes gave way to cassette tapes, the use of recorded speeches became more and more practical. Not only were cassette tapes much less expensive than long-playing records, they could be played almost anywhere, and speeches or testimonials could be recorded with little effort or studio equipment. This was a medium perfectly suited for direct-sales distributorships. The personal stories of successful distributors could be recorded on cassette tapes and put into the hands of other distributors quickly and at a reasonable price, and such taped speeches quickly became commonplace within the Amway world.

What Yager brought to this trend was his awareness that many serious distributors have a virtually unlimited appetite for knowledge, inspiration, and encouragement through tapes. One tape a month wouldn't satisfy the need, Yager realized. Maybe one a week or more, listened to once a day, was needed. Constantly listening to tapes produces a steady stream of positive thought "know-how," business and life training, he argued, and that is a necessity, not a luxury, in building a new business.

Mass Meetings

Large group meetings were similarly important, in Yager's view of things. Conventions shouldn't be once-a-year events but an unending fixture of the distributor's life. Few things are as stimulating as the excitement of a live crowd and few things as reinforcing to one's own dreams as sharing them with fellow dreamers. Achievers feed off the energy of one another, so the more often they meet together, the better.

Amway Corporation staged annual conventions in Grand Rapids, Michigan, from its earlier days and encouraged distributor groups to conduct their own meetings. It could be accurately stated that meetings — of every size and description — are, and always have been, the heart and soul of any Amway business.

But Yager raised the Amway convention to an art form; he quickly grasped the central role of mass gatherings in the business and was the first distributor outside the corporation itself to organize weekend meetings which, within a few years, drew larger crowds than any in the country.

Yager's approach was to develop a skillfully orchestrated calendar of year-round events which brought his distributors together in various combinations. His first major events were staged in Charlotte each autumn. They were his version of Amway's Free Enterprise Day, which drew ten thousand people each year as early as the early 1970s. These events grew and caused several Double Diamonds to have their own capacity crowds in the mid 1970s. By the early 1990s, Yager was filling the seventy-five-thousand-seat Georgia Dome in Atlanta, and within a few years he was forced to decentralize the event, holding it in six separate venues around the country. There was literally no single stadium or coliseum in America large enough to accommodate the one-hundred-thousand-plus who wished to attend.

In addition, some of his largest Diamond leaders had organizations that had also grown beyond any one building's capacity. It is common not only in the U.S.A. but throughout the world to see those in his group holding a dozen or two annual meetings with fifteen thousand distributors in attendance.

In addition to these annual mega-events, Yager's leaders organize hundreds of winter Dream Weekends, summertime Family Reunions, spring Go Diamond conferences, and monthly seminars and rallies too numerous to count.

The planning and execution of these events is obviously a massive task. Putting it all together requires a large team of full-time professionals who have deep pockets and specialized skills. But over the years Yager, as well as some of his more ambitious associates such as Bill Britt, Bill Childers, Don Wilson, and Jerry Meadows, have created staffs and the infrastructure to manage events of this size. To do so, they have invested huge amounts of time and money. The result, however, is a powerful tool for building Amway businesses that pays off for all their distributors.

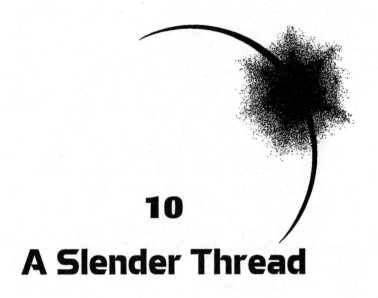

10

A Slender Thread

In the first few years after moving to Charlotte, Dexter Yager showed the Amway plan to hundreds of prospects. Some listened, some yawned, and some understood and got in. But no one saw the full implications of Yager's vision with greater clarity than a thirty-eight-year-old stranger from Chapel Hill, North Carolina, who rang Yager's doorbell one Saturday morning in 1970.

The stranger's name was Bill Britt. He had called Dexter at home the night before. He was calling, he said, on the advice of a man named Dominick Coniguliaro, a mutual friend in New York, who had given him Yager's name and phone number. "Dominick tells me you're involved in a new business," Britt had said on the phone, as he introduced himself. "He told me I should call you, and you'd explain it to me, so that's why I'm calling."

"OK. Come see me, and I'll explain it," Yager said.

"You don't understand," Britt responded. "I live in Chapel Hill. That's a three-hour drive away. I'm a busy man. I have a full-time job, I'm going to graduate school full-time on top of that, and I'm not all that interested anyway, just curious. I don't have time to drive down to Charlotte, so why don't you just explain it to me over the phone?"

"I can't explain it over the phone," said Yager.

Britt wasn't very patient with Yager. "Well, if you can't explain it over the phone, just forget it!"

Yager was pleasant, but he didn't budge. "OK. I'll forget it, then."

OK. End of conversation.

But when Britt hung up the phone and turned back to the television show he was watching, he couldn't get the conversation off his mind. Something nagged at him: *What if there really is something special about this deal?* he worried. *What if I might be missing the boat?*

But no. He had a golf date scheduled for the next morning; he was supposed to be playing with some buddies down at Pinehurst. Besides, he wasn't the kind of guy who chased around after something he knew nothing about. He was a no-nonsense kind of guy, and he was extremely busy, and this fellow Yager had given him no information at all except that he was retired at the age of thirty. So Britt pushed it from his mind and tried to concentrate on the TV show.

But he couldn't forget it. He remembered something else: Yager had told him he was in the top 2 percent income bracket in the country. Maybe he was lying. But still, there was that thing about being retired at thirty. He couldn't be lying about that. *Nah, forget it, I've got no time to fool with it,* he thought.

Back to the television.

But he couldn't forget it. He was curious. He was hungry for some extra income. Charlotte was only three hours away. And he wasn't that eager to play golf anyway. By then a couple of hours had passed, and it was after 11:00 P.M., but Britt picked up the phone, redialed the Charlotte number, and asked Yager if he could come see him the next morning.

Bill Britt was no ordinary prospect. There was no way for either of them to know it at the time, but his encounter with the Amway business in Yager's living room that Saturday morning was the beginning of one of the most productive distributor partnerships in the history of Amway.

Britt was a career professional in municipal government. In 1970, he was serving as the city manager of Goldsboro, North Carolina, a town of about twenty-five thousand people in the metropolitan area of Raleigh-Durham. He was a married, no children, good reputation, perfect health college graduate with a successful career and a typical middle-class lifestyle. And he was very frustrated.

Britt was the oldest child in a family of eight and had grown up in various places up and down the East Coast. His father had a drinking problem, and his inability to handle alcohol kept his family permanently off-balance. They were not poor, but they were always in debt and never put down roots in a single hometown that the Britts could call a permanent home. Bill always worked as a child and teenager, at typical jobs such as bagging groceries and delivering newspapers — the usual stuff. He slid through high school without caring very much about school work, graduated in Daytona Beach, Florida, and moved to New York to work.

College had never been in the picture when Britt was growing up, but he realized he had to find a way to get there. This was in the period just after World War II, when the new G.I. bill was opening college doors for millions of

Americans returning from military service. Bill decided that his best route to college was through the military, so he joined the Army.

The Army did eventually put Britt into college, but before it did that, it gave him something even more valuable: for the first time, he began to realize his potential as a leader and an achiever. He was tapped for officer candidate training, one of only two non-college recruits in a class of sixty-three officer candidates, and finished the training at the top of the class. He was commissioned as a lieutenant and immediately volunteered for combat duty in Korea.

For the deeply patriotic Britt, Korea was a proving ground for his emerging skill and confidence. He served as a combat engineer and commanded the 1,437th Floating Bridge Company. He loved his country and was ready to die for it, but that was not his destiny. Instead, combat sharpened him, as it has done for many young men throughout history, and sent him home primed for something significant.

That significant something did not present itself immediately. Britt first went to college. He graduated with a degree in engineering and became a career government manager. Starting in Raleigh as an assistant city manager, moving on from there, picking up graduate courses as he went along, Britt settled into a comfortable life and career. He was well respected and happily married to a woman named Peggy, but basically unchallenged, his gifts for achievement underutilized.

As he reached his mid-thirties, Britt began to stall out financially. He made a good salary, but he couldn't seem to get ahead. He hungered for more than the average, routine life that might have satisfied others, but he knew that he could never afford his dreams on the income of a municipal employee, even if he was the boss. So he began to look for a business on the side, something he could maintain in addition to his professional career, something to provide a second income.

Twenty-five thousand dollars a year in extra income: That figure emerged as his "best possible case scenario." If he could find some kind of franchise operation or any legitimate entrepreneurial business that would generate an extra twenty-five thousand dollars each year, he figured he would have it made.

As he pursued that goal, he made a terrible decision that indirectly resulted in his arriving at Dexter Yager's doorstep that fateful Saturday morning in 1970. The bad decision he made was an investment decision. As he cast about for ways to get ahead, Britt was persuaded to invest ten thousand dollars in the start-up costs of a new business venture called NabCorps. It sounded good, but he didn't have the ten thousand, so he went to the bank, borrowed the entire amount, and plunged in. He lost every dime. The business deal turned out to be a fraud; the man heading it was a crook who took the money and ran. It was a total fiasco.

Stung by the loss of big money he didn't have, Britt decided to organize other people who had lost money in the scam to try to find a way to recover their money. In this process, he flew to Buffalo, New York, to meet with one of his fellow victims. They eventually concluded that there was no effective legal recourse open to them, and they dropped the effort. When Britt left Buffalo, he realized he had reached a dead end on the investment deal, but he left his business card with the man there, in case additional developments might ever occur in the case.

It was three years later, long after Britt had forgotten about trying to recover his ten grand, that he received a letter, quite unexpectedly, from the Coniguliaro man he had visited in Buffalo. The letter said, in effect, that this fellow had discovered an interesting new business, one that would make their losses in NabCorps seem trivial.

Yeah, right, Britt thought. He wanted nothing to do with it. He wadded the letter up and threw it into the trash can.

That night, the phone rang, and it was the man from Buffalo, urging Britt to listen to his new deal. "OK, tell me about it," Bill said. But it wasn't going to be that easy. "I can't tell you about it," said the voice in Buffalo, "but I'll give you the name of a guy in Charlotte. You call him and he'll tell you all about it."

It was a weird kind of runaround. "Why," Britt asked, "did you call me if you can't tell me anything?" Exasperated with the whole strange conversation, Britt wrote down the name and number Coniguliaro gave him and hung up, never intending to make the call to Charlotte.

In retrospect, it was fortuitous that NBC, CBS, and ABC's television programming was so deadly dull that night, because Britt was bored and restless, and the call from Buffalo had aroused his curiosity, so he picked up the phone and dialed the Charlotte number after all.

By that slender thread, he arrived at Yager's house and left a few hours later, having signed up as an Amway distributor. Yager insisted that Coniguliaro must be his sponsor, according to the Amway policy, but Britt was ready to get started. He took his new distributor kit home to Chapel Hill and spent the next two days dissecting and analyzing the marketing plan, going over every aspect of the operation. He looked for the hidden "gotcha"; he found none. He tried to find a fatal flaw; it wasn't there. He came to a conclusion: *If the products are any good at all, I can make a fortune in this deal.*

And he did. More than twenty-five years later, Bill Britt manages a massive Amway operation that includes dozens of Diamond distributorships all over the world and has made him and others a multimillionaire many times over. He worked closely with Yager for many years, until their two networks of distributors grew so large that it became impractical for them to do business jointly, and they now manage their affairs separately, still only a few hours apart.

The names Yager and Britt are frequently linked when Amway watchers analyze the evolution of the Amway phenomenon. Though Britt now leads his own *system* within Amway, the business-building pattern that he teaches is highly similar to Yager's, emphasizing the key elements of dream building and the use of business tools to keep distributors involved. Like Yager, Britt teaches that a real leader should continue to invest time in the people he sponsors. The result, for each of them, is a huge army of fiercely loyal downline Diamonds who are themselves the leaders of literally tens of thousands of distributors.

Like many men and women who have achieved greatly, Bill Britt has no special explanation to offer which will account for his extraordinary success. "I always worked hard," he says, "but so do lots of other people. I'm not smarter or more talented than most people; what I've done is really no big deal. But I do know this: I never wanted to be average. I just wanted to be Bill Britt, whatever that happened to be, but I knew I wasn't average, and I was determined to keep looking until I found the thing that would let me reach my full potential. And that's what Amway was for me. Sometimes it scares me to think what a slender thread brought me into this business, but I'm thankful I found it, because it has given me the opportunity to became all that God intended for me to be."

11

Hold Fast
to Dreams

Into every life, a little rain must fall. Adversity. It is a common denominator in every success story — every life, every marriage, every growing business. Amway is no exception.

In its earliest days, Amway was such a tiny blip on the American radar screen that no one took the time to shoot at it, certainly not on a national level. For individual distributors, there was the constant need to explain the business to misinformed and frequently critical bystanders. Anything new will be dismissed or even ridiculed until it proves itself, and during the 1960s and 1970s Amway distributors learned to live with the kind of sniping that attends a new business. In fact, they considered it inevitable and rather harmless.

It was not too bad for distributors to be jabbed by an unkind brother-in-law at the family dinner table. It was quite another thing to endure an attack on the legitimacy of one's business that appeared in the morning edition of *USA TODAY* or came up on national television.

Hearing Amway whacked by the next-door neighbor is merely a nuisance; hearing it whacked on network TV by the likes of Mike Wallace or Phil Donahue is true adversity.

Amway began to face such adversity increasingly in the late 1970s and early 1980s as the corporation grew and became a more and more visible part of the national land-scape. What had formerly been considered a quirky little soap company, easily dismissed as a fad, or a door-to-door business of no national importance, was rapidly becoming a household word, and very few people in the general public understood it.

One thing was certain: Whatever Amway was, it was clearly here to stay, and powerful forces in the media and the government began to take notice.

The first challenge, perhaps predictably, came from a federal regulatory agency. The Federal Trade Commission (FTC) is the body responsible for guaranteeing that compa-nies doing business with the American public do so with fairness and integrity. Like most bureaucracies, the FTC has difficulty responding to new and innovative approaches to the marketplace, and the surging growth of Amway in the 1970s caught its attention.

The FTC took one look at the Amway marketing plan and jumped to the conclusion that it was a *pyramid*. A pyra-mid is an elaborate form of business fraud that has been around virtually as long as people have been conducting business. Pyramid schemes seem to flourish particularly well in direct sales and multilevel environments, and their common feature is that a few people make lots of money in the first few years, and those who follow them into the scheme make nothing. Pyramids are, of course, against the law.

There are specific legal ways to define a pyramid, and Amway was not at any time a pyramid by any definition. But it emerged in a period during which a few actual pyramids had been shut down in high-profile legal actions and the leaders indicted and convicted. In at least one instance (Glenn Turner's Dare To Be Great company), the motivational rhetoric and business style seemed similar to that of Amway, and some regulatory watchdogs were inclined to label Amway as yet another scam.

In 1974, the FTC filed a complaint against Amway, and the headlines that accompanied the action set off shock waves throughout the young company. The publicity that Amway was, or might be, a sophisticated flim-flam game was the worst nightmare of a new business whose greatest task was winning the confidence of the public. When the federal government announces that it intends to put a new company under a microscope, there is little middle ground; the ordeal either kills that company or it makes it stronger.

Amway fought back. Rather than conducting a dodge-and-delay strategy, trying to stall government action, or avoiding the charges on legal technicalities, DeVos and Van Andel announced that they and Amway had nothing to hide, that they welcomed the opportunity to explain fully the nature of their business, and that they would provide government investigators total and immediate access to all records and operations of the company.

"We have a solid business," they were saying, "and we hate pyramids more than the FTC does, so let's make this court case an opportunity to show the public exactly what Amway is."

It was a strategic masterstroke. Once they reached the courtroom, the suspicions expressed in the FTC complaint evaporated. There was simply nothing there. The proceedings ended with the government presenting Amway with a gift it could never have gained otherwise: official validation of the integrity of its marketing plan.

After months of hearings, the judge for the Federal Trade Commission issued a ruling that affirmed Amway so emphatically, it may as well have been written by the Amway public relations staff: "The Amway sales and marketing plan is not a pyramid plan. In less than twenty years, it has built a substantial manufacturing company and an efficient distribution *system,* which has brought new products into the market...Consumers are benefited by this new source of supply and have responded by remarkable brand loyalty to Amway products."

Thus the first major challenge to Amway as it began to establish itself as a serious national business came from the government and turned out to be more a blessing than a curse.

The next challenge came from the national news media. Once again, the very fact that Amway would face the questions of the national press was a testimony to its rapidly growing size and strength. NBC, CBS, and ABC do not concern themselves with minor players in the national drama. Mike Wallace and Phil Donahue rarely waste air time on little businesses unknown to the public. But by the early 1980s, Amway was becoming a national phenomenon, impossible to ignore.

Those were the golden years of the CBS television show *Sixty Minutes,* an investigatory news program which for several years was the most highly rated show on television. *Sixty Minutes* featured Mike Wallace, a tough reporter who regularly roasted the subjects of his reports with an attack-dog interview technique which, given his huge audience, could break reputations literally overnight. One journalist, Gary Paul Gates, observed that "CBS management made sure that the four most dreaded words in the

English language are 'Mike Wallace is here.'"

Inevitably, as Amway grew, *Sixty Minutes* took notice. The company was still little understood by mainstream America, and many misconceptions about it seemed to be taking hold in the public mind. In 1982 the CBS team, led by Mike Wallace himself, informed Amway officials in Michigan that it would be doing a full investigative report and that the team would focus not only on the corporate story, but also on the story of an individual distributor who would come to hear those four dreaded words, "Mike Wallace is here."

That distributor turned out to be Dexter Yager.

Amway Corporation itself was the primary target, and Van Andel and DeVos prepared to face television's Grim Reaper. Once again, as they had with the FTC, the partners defended themselves by flinging open the doors and inviting Wallace and his CBS crew to take a long, hard look. "We have nothing to hide; we have much of which to be proud; come, bring your cameras; do your best."

Not that the partners took anything for granted. They hired a New York consultant, Walter Pfister, a former vice president of *ABC News,* to prepare them for the *Sixty Minutes* interviews. Pfister had made a tidy career of helping corporate executives, who are generally unaccustomed to television cameras, prepare to put their best foot forward when Mike Wallace and similar investigators came to call.

Wallace interviewed DeVos and Van Andel, snooped around the Ada corporate headquarters, and seemed satisfied that things were unexpectedly on the up-and-up. He seemed impressed by what he saw and heard and acknowledged it. But the story was not complete, not until he had visited Yager on his home turf and had seen one of Yager's gigantic motivational rallies for himself. He packed his cameras and headed for Charlotte just in time to experience a famous rip-roaring Free Enterprise Celebration.

Yager learned first from an Amway corporate friend that he was Wallace's primary target. "I told them I didn't want to do it. I just wasn't interested, but they told me there *was* no choice. It was going to happen, one way or another, so I agreed to cooperate. They gave me Mike Wallace's phone number in New York, and I talked to him. He told me he wasn't out to do a hatchet job on Amway — he just wanted to get the true picture of things — and I believed him."

Once it was clear that *Sixty Minutes* was locked in on Yager, the corporation sent its outside consultants, who had coached DeVos and Van Andel, to Charlotte to prepare Dex and Birdie. "They just went over basic stuff with us, like look at the camera, don't let your eyes wander, call Mike Wallace by his name, that sort of thing. They said not to sit back in your chair when the cameras are running, because on TV that makes it look like you're sliding away from the question. That sort of thing."

Wallace and his crew came to Charlotte on the weekend of Yager's Free Enterprise Celebration and shot dozens of hours of video over a three-day period. He did interviews with both the Yagers, toured their home and estate, and roamed freely around the coliseum during the weekend rally including backstage and through the crowd. As expected, much of the footage that eventually aired on CBS emphasized the huge crowds and the emotional pitch of the rally. The Yager strategy was to be as open as possible, conceal nothing, and let the chips fall where they may. "I let him into my life," Yager explains. "I poured my heart out, and I was as honest as if he had been my brother. I just tried to be totally fair."

The approach turned out to be a smart one. Despite the program's reputation for brutally negative reporting, and despite the apparent *Sixty Minutes* preconception that Amway crowds were a bunch of out-of-control yahoos, the report, when it finally aired, four months later was fairly balanced and moderate in tone. The overall impact was a positive one, if only because Wallace did *not* load up his big guns and blow Amway off the map.

If a company is somewhat new and fighting an image problem with the general public and *Sixty Minutes* targets it, the ability to survive that intense scrutiny before tens of millions of viewers becomes a major public relations boost. That was the outcome of Amway's experience. Yager explains it this way: "I guess when you hear that somebody is going to beat the heck out of you, that they're going to take off your arms and legs and shoot you, and that they're going to cut you all up and sell you for hamburger, and then all they do is break off your fingernail, you feel pretty excited about it. And it really doesn't matter at that point when your friends tell you, 'But you had perfect nails!'"

The national exposure did much to establish Amway as a force to be reckoned with in the American marketplace and to affirm the Yagers as its most prominent leaders. "When I watched the show that night, I had mixed emotions. I'm not sure what I expected, and I was afraid we hadn't come off too well. But when I was back in Rome, New York, I went into this little Italian restaurant and bar and the bartender recognized me and told me, 'Hey, you looked real good; you came across real good.' I asked him how he felt about the other stuff, the critical stuff from other people they interviewed. 'Aw, I don't care anything about that. Doesn't matter.' He just waved it off. What he remembered was that we were there, and we had a great lifestyle to show for all our hard work, and Mike Wallace and CBS treated us with respect like serious people with a serious business. That's what mattered."

Apparently, the bartender's reaction was generally shared across the country. And in the end, even Mike Wallace publicly expressed his admiration for Amway based on what he learned in the process of investigating it. In an interview with Larry King, he acknowledged that he had entered the project with "preconceived" ideas about Amway which he later found to be "misconceptions." When King asked him about his investigation, he joked, "This is going to sound like a commercial for Amway," so positive were his comments. "We thought we would have to do the story without cooperation, but these are classy people. They opened up to us...These people are first-rate."

Ted Koppel, the star of the ABC television network news department, was also curious about Amway when he interviewed Wallace on a later occasion. Wallace described the tendency of many companies to resist and deflect his CBS reporters: "I think a business serves itself much better by being forthcoming...Let me give you examples...The Amway Corporation felt they had something to gain by making the best case that they could. They didn't ask for questions ahead of time; they didn't ask for any special editing privileges. They were forthcoming. They opened their books; they opened their plants to us. And as a result, you can talk to these people, and they'll say, 'Perhaps it wasn't the broadcast that we would have liked to see, but it was fair, it was balanced, it was accurate, and we probably did ourselves good in the long run.'"

No question about it. Amway is built on a dream, and a dream is an easy thing for an uninformed public to misunderstand. Whether in the earliest days with Van Andel and DeVos, or in the development of Yager's own business, or in the mind of the newest distributor, one of the critical tasks of Amway is to keep the dream alive in the face of misconceptions and the criticism of others. The scrutiny of *Sixty Minutes,* like the challenge of the FTC, had the potential to damage or derail the growing enterprise. But in each case, and many more like it, the Amway dream was too tough, too sturdy. It survived; it became stronger; it was a dream that would not die.

12

Bitter
or Better

However vexing Amway's challenges might have been, they pale in comparison to the flesh-and-blood adversity that individual Amway distributors have faced as they build their businesses.

When a company faces adversity in the form of a lawsuit or a public relations problem, it can test the company's resilience, but the challenge is at least impersonal and temporary.

On the other hand, a family can awaken one morning to find itself suddenly facing adversity so devastating, so soul-jarring, that it makes lawsuits and public relations problems seem trivial by comparison. Why do bad things happen to good people? There may never be an adequate answer to that age-old question. But when disaster strikes, and life itself is on the line, sheer survival can become so difficult that nothing else matters, and a person's dreams can be the first thing to die.

Dexter Yager himself knows adversity. In the fall of 1986, he was flattened by a massive stroke. His right side was completely paralyzed, he was rushed to an intensive care unit, and the most optimistic prognosis was that he would survive but never walk again. It was the beginning of a tough, painful year of rehabilitation, one small bit of progress at a time, until Dex eventually had a miraculous full recovery.

Don and Nancy Wilson faced an even more difficult kind of adversity. Their lives changed dramatically and permanently in a single split second on June 29, 1993, plunging them into a crisis so grave that it could kill almost anyone's dreams.

Anyone who ever met the Wilsons would agree that they epitomize the ideal Amway success story. They are an energetic, friendly, attractive couple who took to the Amway business like a child takes to an ice cream cone.

The Wilsons had been college sweethearts back in New England in the 1960s. They both worked their way through college, marrying halfway through undergraduate school, and moved to Vermont to settle into the professional roles they had always wanted — he, a high school teacher and basketball coach; she a nurse. They lived in small towns, first in Vermont, then in Maine, and both were good at what they did — Don, in fact, had just won coach-of-the-year honors the year before they saw the Amway plan.

But they soon realized that the rewards of coaching and nursing left them short of the financial security and lifestyle of which they had dreamed. They both had successful careers, but they were frustrated. And then along came Amway. Boom! When the Wilsons' business began to grow, they were able to replace both their incomes, leave their jobs, and eventually, in 1988, leave New England to build their dream home in Ogden, Utah. From there, they continued raising their family of three children, directed one of the largest Diamond distributorships in the nation, and enjoyed all the perks and benefits of the millionaires which they had become.

On the last weekend in June 1993 they hosted one of those weekend conferences for which the Amway business is so famous. This occasion brought together one of their personal downline groups — about four thousand people in all — to the Bally's Hotel in Las Vegas. It was a festive, happy weekend. The guest speakers were the Yagers; music was provided by a singing group from Lee College in Tennessee, where daughter Jenny was scheduled to attend as a freshman in the fall; the celebrated Oak Ridge Boys performed for the crowd on Sunday morning. It was a magical, emotional weekend.

On Tuesday morning, Don and Nancy waved the last of their guests goodbye and drove southward to San Bernardino, California, to meet an architect who was designing a log cabin for them to build on their lake property in Utah. He wanted them to see a similar cabin that was under construction in San Bernardino. "We felt great on the drive out to California that morning," Don remembers. "We were relaxed and excited about life."

As they prowled through the construction site, commenting on this and that aspect of the cabin design, they came to an open stairwell, with stairs and handrails still incomplete. Steve, the architect, paused before heading up the stairs and asked Don and Nancy if they could manage the climb. Sure, they said, and started up the stairs.

No one is sure exactly what happened next. Nancy stumbled. She reached out instinctively for a handrail that was not there. Her body pitched over the edge, falling toward a concrete floor a story-and-a-half below. Don heard her gasp; he turned and in a split second saw her lying, sprawling, on the floor below. The rest is something of a blur, remembered thousands of times, but always with the same unreal rush of impressions: she was conscious; he held her, prayed with her, comforted her, and waited for the ambulance that Steve had run to call.

Only Nancy could sense how gravely injured she was. "I can't breathe," she told Don in answer to his questions. She had broken seven ribs and punctured her diaphragm, and her thoracic organs had been shoved up into her lungs, compressing them. And there was more: She asked Don to put her legs down. He could see they were already down and in a very unnatural position. He could do little but hold her and pray.

"She looked at me and said calmly, 'Honey, I'm gonna die.' She was absolutely at peace, not panic-stricken, almost matter-of-fact about it," Don recalls. "'Honey, I'm gonna die,' just like that, and the wonderful thing is that she was so at peace with her God and so ready to go if that was His will."

But it was not Nancy Wilson's time. The ambulance arrived, finally, and rushed her to a trauma center, keeping her alive despite a shattered backbone and a severed spinal cord. The medical team took her immediately into surgery, warning Don that she may or may not survive. Don called his children, called his pastor, and immediately notified some of his Amway friends.

After an endless wait outside the operating room, the surgeon emerged to report that Nancy had survived the immediate crisis but that she had some paralysis and needed more surgery on her back. From there she went to another hospital, another operating room, and Don endured another night-long vigil. Again, a surgeon emerged with a mixed report: "Mr. Wilson," he said soberly, "we've put her together the best we can, but she has no feeling from the waist down."

"What does that mean, exactly?" Don insisted.

The doctor paused. "It means," he said slowly, "that we've done all we can do humanly. Anything else from this point on will have to be a miracle from God."

The final chapter is not yet written in Nancy Wilson's story of remarkable courage and faith. But in the years since that fateful trip to California on June 29, 1993, she and her family have walked a long path of pain and fortitude of struggle and overcoming grace that is still inspiring the hundreds of thousands of people who know them and who have watched their faith operate under such terrible pressure.

For the next eighteen months, she lived with an open incision in her back, which originally ran from her waist to her shoulder blades, created by the need to implant surgically in her back the steel rods that would do the work of her shattered spine. She endured infections, repeated surgeries, and all sorts of medical complications, major and minor. Perhaps worst of all, she faced bad news about her paralysis — no further progress, not yet — and the need to learn to function in a wheelchair, with no way of knowing when or if that situation would end.

Through it all, Don and Nancy Wilson have refused to lose their optimism and hopeful spirit. One will find no bitterness or self-pity in the Wilson household. To the contrary, even her hospital room was the most positive place in the hospital, one person remarked. "I think the doctors and nurses themselves came in when they needed a lift! She is so strong that when people come to encourage her, she winds up encouraging them!"

There is more than Amway-style positive thinking at work here; there is also the Wilsons' rock-solid spiritual faith. No one who knows the story of their ordeal can doubt that their God is far more to them than a concept; their strength in this trial testifies more powerfully than any sermon to the reality of a personal spiritual experience.

Someone described it this way: "I've heard it said that believing in God is just an emotional crutch. Well, if that's what Nancy has, all I can say is, give me two of them, brother! Whatever she's got is good enough for me!"

And what happened to the Wilsons' Amway business during the 2 years plus of her recovery when Don dropped everything to be by her side? Not only did it not collapse; it actually grew, at a strong, constant rate, and the income never stopped.

Throughout the ordeal, the Wilsons got strong support from Amway corporate officers in Michigan. Several weeks after the accident, they asked Don, "Isn't there *anything* we can do for Nancy?" They had asked before, and Don had always responded, "Just pray for her." But this time he had a suggestion: The Yager organization had planned a giant Free Enterprise Celebration in Atlanta's Georgia Dome for Labor Day weekend. Seventy-five thousand distributors would be there, most of whom knew Nancy and had been praying for her.

"Nancy would love to be in Atlanta for the celebration," Don said. It would require leasing a private jet, a specially-fitted air ambulance, to get her from Salt Lake City to Atlanta and back.

"Do you suppose...?," Don wondered.

"Of course," Amway president Dick DeVos responded.

And it was done. Perhaps only a company that understands dreams would have made such a gesture. And only a woman of Nancy Wilson's courage would have cared. But when the spotlights hit the stage in Atlanta, Nancy was there, and her presence electrified the huge audience.

Speaking to the packed coliseum, a microphone placed beside her wheelchair, she tried to provide a bit of perspective: "Our life changed, and we don't know why. There is no good answer. It's just one of those things that happens."

Only God knows why bad things happen to good people. But it takes no genius to realize that, when they happen in a situation like the Wilsons', the Amway business makes an enormous difference. After her accident, cards, letters, and gifts poured into the Wilson home — the secretaries quit counting at twenty thousand! Amway friends from around the world rushed to support them with prayer and work. "The support of the Amway people kept me going," Nancy says.

And there was the money. When life hangs in the balance, money seems unimportant, but in the several-year struggle to recover from such a devastating injury, the financial resources from the Wilsons' Amway business made a huge difference. Because of those resources, Nancy could get the best care, she could have her family with her, and she could deal with her injuries without worrying about being wiped out financially.

"If this had happened before Amway, while I was coaching, it would have been every American family's worst financial nightmare," Don reflects. "It happens every day. One minute you're OK, and the next minute you're financially ruined forever. Thank God for Amway, because it put us in a position not to have to worry about that. Does Amway still matter to us, after all this? Absolutely. More now than ever."

The Wilsons have built a new home in Arizona, fully equipped for a wheelchair-bound lady of the house. They are still leading a growing Amway business, with the added impact of their experience: They have been through the fire, and it has not consumed them. Their faith is intact, and so is their attitude toward the future. They found a dream in the Amway business, and when adversity had taken its best shot, it was a dream that would not die.

"I decided," Nancy once said, "that I could either get bitter or get better. I chose to get better."

13

Dreams

Animals are capable of thinking: They use logic, they remember, and they solve problems. They even experience emotion. Anyone who owns a favorite pet will testify that animals can express love and miss people who are gone and show happiness or sorrow.

But animals don't dream. They lack the spiritual equipment to do so. Dreaming is uniquely human. It is more than emotion, and it is more than thought. The power to dream goes beyond logic or even feeling; it lies very close to the heart of what it means to be human, to be made in the image of God.

If dreams are uniquely human, it is also true that they are as distinctive and as individual as people themselves.

Dreams are as individual as fingerprints. Dreams are uniquely human; dogs and horses don't dream. No two people dream alike. Two people may share a dream; they may agree to dream together of the same thing; but every individual dreams in a private and protected place, deep within the heart, a place that cannot be entered or owned by another.

Our dreams are our own, and they express who and what we are. Thus, Anne Frank in the 1940s could live secretly in a crowded attic in Amsterdam and dream of being free, and all the Nazis in the world could not take her dream from her. They could storm the attic and drag her into a concentration camp and eventually kill her, but they could not keep her from scribbling her dreams into a schoolgirl's diary so that fifty years later they still inspire and uplift people who read them.

Similarly, a middle-aged seamstress named Rosa Parks in the 1950s could sit on a public bus in Montgomery, Alabama, way in the back where black people were required to ride, and she could dream of being respected and treated with dignity. All the racist laws in the state and all the angry bus drivers could humiliate her, but they could not steal her dream, until finally that dream burst through to ignite the modern civil rights movement.

Dreams are as individual as snowflakes. No two in the world are alike. But like snowflakes, dreams can be fragile things if they are not nurtured and kept alive. When a dream dies, something fundamentally human is lost, and the best part of living is lost with it. "Hold fast to dreams," wrote the poet Langston Hughes, "for if dreams die, life is a broken-winged bird that cannot fly."

The dreams of many Amway people are often expressed in the form of material things — cars, houses, boats, expensive jewelry and glamorous vacations — symbols of success that are easy to recognize. Talking of these things becomes almost a cliché in the Amway world. To speak of owning a

Amway cofounders Rich DeVos and Jay Van Andel

DeVos and Van Andel in the late 1940s, when they started a flight school as one of their first business ventures

©Amway Corporation

Among the many incentives for high-achieving distributors is the reward of being guests on the corporate yacht, *Enterprise V.*

©Amway Corporation

Peter Island, in the British Virgin Islands, is owned by Amway Corporation and is used as a getaway for top-level distributors.

Amway's mile-long world headquarters now has building space in excess of 10 million square feet, a staff totaling more than 13,000, and supports over 2.5 million distributorships in more than 70 countries and territories.

The DeVos and Van Andel Families

Bottom Row, L-R: Rich DeVos, cofounder and former president; Steve Van Andel, chairman; Dick DeVos, president; Jay Van Andel, cofounder and senior chairman.

Top Row, L-R: Cheri DeVos Vander Weide, vice president–corporate affairs; Dave Van Andel, senior vice president–operations; Doug DeVos, senior vice president and managing director–North America; Nan Van Andel, vice president–catalog and communications; Dan DeVos, vice president–corporate affairs; Barb Van Andel-Gaby, vice president–corporate affairs.

Dexter and Birdie Yager, leaders of one of Amway's largest and most successful distributorships, the InterNET system

Dexter Yager's family includes seven children, their spouses, and fifteen grandchildren, many of whom are pictured above.

The Yagers pose for their new direct distributor photo in January 1965.

The InterNET organization now operates from these modern facilities in Charlotte, North Carolina.

Gigantic meetings are a trademark of the InterNET system, bringing in crowds like these of 75,000 distributors in Atlanta's Georgia Dome (above) and 25,000 in Charlotte, North Carolina (below).

The Yagers frequently entertain friends whose names and faces are known around the world. Here Dexter shares a moment with former President Ronald Reagan, a family friend since the 1970s.

Author Charles Paul Conn has been a frequent talk-show guest when the media wants to know about Amway. Here he and Yager appear on a local Charlotte television show in 1982.

diamond ring or a fur coat becomes a kind of code, a short-hand way of saying, "I'm dreaming of a day when I'm free to have what I want, without looking at the price tags." The diamond or the fur itself is not the dream; the freedom is the dream, and the expensive trinkets are merely symbols of it.

To understand how powerfully the Amway opportunity motivates intelligent people, one must understand the freedom that Amway income can buy. In virtually every case, the dreams that push people out of their comfort zones and into the Amway business are tied to freedom of some sort.

For Jim and Arlene Nealis, the dream that drew them into Amway was freedom to slow down and enjoy life. They were not attracted by money — they had lots of that — but by the possibility of having the time to spend and enjoy it.

Jim was a medical doctor, a neurologist. He had grown up in a blue-collar home in New York City; his dad was a cop, and Jim knew from an early age that his ticket to the good life was his smarts. He was an excellent student with a taste for academic achievement that put him on a track for medical school. After earning his M.D. degree at the University of Miami, Nealis moved up to the Ivy League, completing his residency at Columbia University. He then spent a couple of years teaching at the Harvard School of Medicine before moving to Jacksonville, Florida, to start a private practice in neurology.

He was successful — maybe too successful. Within a few years he had a booming practice and all the symbols of financial success: He and Arlene lived in a seventy-five-hundred-square-foot house, drove a Porsche, sailed a thirty-eight-foot yacht, and enjoyed a typical high-income lifestyle. The problem was that they had no time to enjoy it. In fact, they had almost no time together at all.

"I worked a hundred hours many weeks," Jim says. "I would go day after day, always on call, always living by my beeper. One time I went seven months without a night off. I remember driving past a cemetery one time, and thinking, *Well, if I were in there, at least I could get a good night's sleep without this beeper going off!*

Jim and Arlene were raising a family of five children, and Daddy's absence from home weighed heavily on both of them. "When James Jr. was having his fifth birthday party, something came up," Jim recalls, "and I told Arlene I couldn't make it. She asked me, 'Do you realize you have missed every one of his birthday parties for five years!' And it was true. I just wasn't there."

Arlene increasingly felt the pressure. They had what they had worked for during those long years of medical school, but what good was it if they could never enjoy it together? Arlene remembers looking with envy at her less prosperous neighbors. "One time I parked in front of this little house with a white picket fence. It was tiny. But it looked like a house where there was a happy family inside, and I just sat there and bawled. I was thinking, *This is not a very big house, but I wonder if at least they sit down and eat dinner together at night.* That was something we could never do."

When a friend showed up at the Nealis residence late one night to show Jim the plan, Jim's primary motivation for trying the business was his dream of having time for his wife and kids, the dream of getting out of the work trap he had so carefully built for himself. When he began building the business, he took flak from the predictably skeptical bystanders in the medical profession. The skepticism sometimes bordered on outright ridicule.

Rather than killing his dream, the criticism deepened Jim's determination to do whatever it took to succeed in this unlikely venture. He and Arlene reached their first goal — a Diamond-level business — while he was still engaged in full-time medical practice. Today they have the best of both worlds: more income than ever before, with the freedom to enjoy it together and to participate in the lives of their growing children.

Owned by the Air Force

Bill and Peggy Florence had a problem similar to that of Jim and Arlene Nealis. They had worked hard and achieved a level of professional success, but they were unable to enjoy the fruits of their labor because they were virtually owned by their employers.

Bill's employer was Uncle Sam. He was an Air Force pilot, flying C-141 jets from a base in Charleston, South Carolina. Bill was a graduate of Georgia Tech, with a degree in aeronautical engineering; Peggy had a master's degree in education from the University of Georgia and taught school.

Bill loved flying, but he was totally frustrated with the rigid bureaucracy of the U.S. Air Force. "They owned me. I literally could not travel more than sixty miles from home without getting their permission. And then, on top of that, it seemed that in the military no one could make a decision. I was frustrated and unhappy, so I planned to leave the Air Force and go to work as a commercial pilot."

Unfortunately, the oil embargo of the early 1970s coincided with Bill's decision to go to work for a commercial airline. Air travel slumped, airlines began losing money, and pilots were laid off in large numbers. Bill was told his chances of being hired as a commercial pilot within the next several years were virtually nonexistent.

"I was totally depressed. The door was slammed in my face. Being a commercial pilot was all I had worked for, and I was being blocked from that goal due to something that was entirely outside my control."

Meanwhile, Peggy had her own misery. She was teaching a large special education class in a rural school system with insufficient materials and a classroom located in a trailer. It seemed to her that it was impossible to do her job in a truly meaningful way, and she was unhappy. "I cried every morning. I prayed, 'Lord, there's got to be something more. This is not what my life is supposed to be about.'"

It was in their unhappy condition that the Florences saw the Amway plan. "I decided to get in within about ten minutes," Bill says. "I saw the numbers and knew they would work. I was an engineer. I knew how to believe in a system, and I could see that this thing would work. I got in on a Tuesday night, went to my first rally the next Saturday night, and listened to tapes all the way there and back. We left that first rally excited, and we've been excited ever since."

The days of being owned by the Air Force seem long ago to the Florences, who in the early 1990s became some of the top distributor leaders in Amway. They named their two sons Rich and Jay and their daughter Hope. They consider the day they joined the business — not the day they earned their college degrees or the day he received his officer's commission — as the day their future began, and who could argue?

Today Bill still enjoys being a pilot, but it is his own plane that he flies, only one of the elements of a lavish lifestyle made possible by their Amway income as well as by that from several other businesses. Like many Diamonds, the Florences have parlayed their Amway money into a diverse set of investments. A large automobile dealership and a development company are now part of the Florences' income-producing assets. The total package barely resembles the simple Amway distributorship with which it all began.

Pizza Man

Bert Gulick's dream was a bit more basic than the professional frustrations of Jim Nealis and Bill Florence. He was working as hard as he knew how, and yet he was chronically in debt and always broke; he wanted to make more money. Period.

Gulick and his wife, Terri, were typical of millions of young American couples. At the ages of twenty-six and twenty-one, respectively, they were newlyweds with jobs that paid just enough to keep them above the poverty line, but never enough to get ahead. Bert managed two pizza parlors, and Terri worked in a women's clothing store.

They worked hard and asked for no sympathy, but the facts were plain: They lived in a tiny house, drove old beat-up cars, and owed for everything they "owned." "Actually," Bert explains, "we didn't own anything. The bank owned our cars, Sears owned the dishes and the kitchen appliances, Montgomery Ward owned the bedroom suite, Thorp Credit owned Terri's engagement diamond, and VISA and MasterCard owned everything else."

They were determined to get out of debt. They wrote all their debt down on three-by-six-inch note cards and taped them to the bathroom mirror. The debt weighed heavily on their minds. "We felt like we were in bondage," Terri explains, "but there didn't seem to be any way to get out. We were already working so many hours that we rarely had a night off, much less a night out."

The high-income lifestyle that the Gulicks now enjoy as Executive Diamonds was not even on their radar screen when they signed up as distributors twenty years ago. Their dream was simple and honest: to get out of debt. Once that was achieved, their pattern of success in Amway had already been established, and the really impressive rewards have come as a matter of course.

The Gulicks have been especially skillful in developing profitable distributorships outside the United States. In the past half-dozen years, they have traveled to some twenty countries to work with their downline distributors, which now operate in thirty-three countries in Europe, Asia, and Latin America.

Back in his pizza days, Bert Gulick had never traveled abroad; he and Terri didn't even have passports. They had no need for them. Today it is not unusual, in any given year, for their schedule to take Bert and Terri to Hong Kong or Singapore, Italy or Germany, Trinidad or Costa Rica.

Your Own Private Island

Some of the dreams that Amway has brought to reality are concrete and specific — like owning one's own island. When Don and Ruth Storms became distributors, they would never have thought of such a thing, much less dreamed that it could be theirs.

The Storms have been married forty-two years and have seen each of their children follow them into the Amway business with direct distributorships of their own. Originally from the Northeast, they started their Amway business after they moved to Charlotte and met Dexter Yager. The Yagers gave them hope, they say. "I can always remember the four magic words he used to say to us, 'You can do it.' We didn't believe it at the time, but gradually we began to believe it, and when we did, we began to dream."

After the Storms' business grew into a huge Diamond distributorship, but before it made possible the typical stuff like expensive homes and airplanes, the Storms began to dream about owning a place on a lake in New Hampshire. "We used to go there every year with our family," Don tells. "We always had a wonderful family time there, so we began thinking that maybe we could buy a little dream cottage there somewhere. At first we thought about just a tiny cottage for six or seven thousand dollars. Then we began to dream bigger, and we looked at a place for $125,000. As our business and our income grew, our dream grew, too. One summer, a realtor told us about an entire island for sale in Lake Winnipesaukee. We packed a picnic lunch and went out to the island, and while we were there, our kids carved their names in a birch tree and told me, 'Dad, this is *our* island!'

"Now, that was really dreaming! So we bought it. It had a little A-frame cottage on it, just a shack, really, with no indoor plumbing. It was pathetic to look at, much less live in! But we could picture ourselves there. And we kept dreaming."

Today, the Storms own the entire island. The old cottage is gone, and in its place they have built a half-million-dollar house, with twenty-five-hundred square feet of wraparound porches filled with old-fashioned rocking chairs. They also put in a private beach. And to get them back and forth to the mainland, they bought a boat, which was named *Dreamer.* Of course.

The challenge, now, is finding time to visit their island retreat, given the large array of other expensive toys that the Storms can now enjoy. And when they do find time to go to New Hampshire, they make the trip in style, traveling in luxury on their private jet or in a motor coach, or in one of many expensive vehicles. They pay for all those options with a strong income from their Amway business and other diversified investments, including a profitable construction company that Amway dollars spawned.

Now You See It; Now You Don't

As tangible as an island is, that's just how intangible a thing called security is. Most professional men and women list job security as one of their most valued dreams, and Louie Carrillo thought he had a lock on job security. He was a professional air traffic controller at the Miami International Airport, a GS-14 federal employee whose job seemed as secure as any could ever be. He had won numerous awards from the Federal Aviation Administration, was an instructor for less experienced controllers, and was totally committed to his work.

But all that changed abruptly and permanently in 1981 when an illegal government strike was called, and an impasse was reached between the air traffic controllers and President Reagan. Suddenly the job disappeared into thin air, along with his forty-six-thousand-dollar annual income and all the security that Carillo thought went along with it.

He was a ten-year veteran who had an excellent professional track record. But his experience and record suddenly meant nothing.

Little wonder that the Carillo dream was independence and security — real security, the kind that can't be yanked away. They found it as Amway distributors. The Carillos admit that before the bruising strike and unemployment of late 1981, they would not have stooped to look at the Amway plan, but after several months of menial labor and mounting bills, they were ready to look, and they tackled the business with an exceptional level of commitment almost from the beginning. It's amazing sometimes how open one's eyes can become when your back is pushed against the wall.

What is taken for granted one day can become a cherished dream the next day. Now that the trauma of 1981 is in the past, the Carillos are quick to say that their sudden unemployment was a blessing in disguise; it stripped them of a false and illusory security and then pointed them toward one that will last.

There is a type of security, however, even more fundamental than job security, and that is the stability offered by a loving relationship. The sudden loss of a job is not nearly as severe a blow to one's security as the unexpected loss of someone you love. This is perhaps the universal nightmare — the fear that a spouse might be abruptly taken by death.

Helen Huebner has faced that nightmare and survived it.

Helen and her husband Bert were Canadian distributors who built a very large business that became their full-time careers and gave them financial independence as well as a lifestyle they enjoyed with their four children.

But the life they built together was shattered in 1979 when Bert was killed in an automobile accident. In the years that followed, Helen learned that Bert's investment in their Amway business continued to pay off long after he was gone. Helen was able to deal with the grief of her loss without the additional loss of financial security that so many widows face. The business they built together has thrived under Helen's leadership, and as a Double Diamond, she is today one of Canada's most respected Amway leaders.

Bert and Helen shared a dream of financial security. It is one of the greatest testimonies to the Amway *system* that when Bert died, his dream did not die with him.

Helen's is not the only story of this kind of security, as evidenced by those of other Amway leaders such as Nancy Stouffer, Carol Larrimore, Nadine Dodd, Chris Costa, Millie Morales and many Diamond men who have lost their spouses and business partners.

14

The Man
From Hildebrand

Bill Childers is a compact man. He is not large, but the overall impression in meeting him is not that he is small but that he is a person of substance; he is not to be trifled with. He has a look of experience and street-smarts. He appears tough and wiry, all muscle and little body fat, no part of him wasted.

The sign on Bill Childers seems to say: "Don't mess with me. I may not be big, but I am 100 percent man, and if you mess with me, I will whip you six ways to Sunday."

Childers is one of the most successful leaders in the world of Amway. He leads an organization that developed within the Yager tradition for nearly fifteen years but which is now largely independent of any leadership but his own.

"I really respect Dex and Rich DeVos and Jay Van Andel and all the people who brought this business where it is," he says, "but the time came when my organization needed to develop its own identity, and it was my responsibility to step up and be the leader."

No one who knows Childers was surprised that he could do just that. "Every now and then," Dexter Yager explains, "someone comes along, like Bill Britt or Bill Childers, who has the gift of leadership, and the smartest thing for anyone to do is to step aside and let them lead."

Childers is a native North Carolinian from the tiny town of Hildebrand. He came from a working-class family with a father who aspired to own his own business and who eventually failed to reach his goals through a combination of his own weaknesses and the unreliability of his business partners. "We were salt-of-the-earth people," Bill recalls. "But my dad never was satisfied to just work for someone else. He would work all day in the textile mill and then work at night building his own mill. He knew the only way to make it big was to have his own business."

Bill's father's dream was to build his own textile company, and some of Bill's earliest memories were working with him in the evenings to build a textile mill. But eventually the dream of the elder Childers collapsed; he became overly dependent on alcohol to relieve the stress of his life, and as the pressure increased, so did his use of alcohol. Then his troubles compounded: He was injured in an automobile accident, suffered a heart attack, and ultimately became unable to stay atop all his business responsibilities. When he was down, struggling, his business associates abandoned him, and his son Bill recalls: "They took advantage of his situation to take his business away from him. He had to sell the mill for a fraction of what it was worth. He lost his health and his business, and there was nothing we could do about it."

THE DREAM THAT WILL NOT DIE

The young Bill Childers, who had worked alongside his father through the night on many occasions, never forgot how his dad's dreams of owning a business were lost. His memories undoubtedly contributed to his passion for the Amway business when that opportunity arose.

First, there was college and the military. Childers was an outstanding football player, one of those athletes who plays at a level well beyond what his size and sheer talent would indicate. He played football at the University of Nebraska, one of the nation's premier football powers, in the Big Eight Conference, far away from his home in North Carolina. But his heart never left Hildebrand, and when his father became gravely ill midway through Bill's third collegiate year, he returned home.

The elder Childers died, and Bill never returned to college. He married and soon after was drafted into the Army. The next step was a familiar one to his Vietnam generation: basic training in Georgia in the summertime. Hot. Miserable. Living in a cramped two-room apartment near Fort Gordon, followed by the same situation in Fort Hood, Texas.

It was 1964, and Pfc. Bill Childers was not a happy soldier. His salary was $195 a month. He and his young wife were far from home. She was pregnant. And he had orders to ship out to Vietnam just as the war was heating up and the body bags were beginning to pile up. Only five days before he was due to ship out to Vietnam, his Protestant chaplain learned that Bill's wife was large with child, and he had his combat orders rescinded. He was pulled out of the line and didn't go. The baby was born the next week — a nine-pound, eight-ounce boy who was named Billy. Uncle Sam had little desire to send fathers to the war zone, and soon Bill was given an honorable release from the Army.

It was back home to Carolina, then, and time to go for

his slice of the American pie. Bill first applied for a job with a big corporation. That seemed the best path to the good life. In his case, the company was National Cash Register, and it was his first hint that the great corporate success story was mostly a mirage. After leaving NCR, he changed jobs several times and did very well, making good salaries and earning positive career reviews. But the treadmill was obviously leading nowhere. The harder he worked, the farther he seemed from his goals. He began to notice that the guys who were on the corporate ladder *above* him, the ones whose jobs he coveted, were no better off than he was. They were no more independent and had no better lifestyles than he did.

For the first time in his life, Bill Childers began to feel trapped. He began to look forward to the weekends, to the parties and the drinking. Then he began to drink *without* waiting for the weekends. "I was the Pabst Blue Ribbon kid," he recalls. "The harder I worked, the more miserable I was. I was going nowhere, and I knew it, and it was eating my guts out."

Childers was smart enough to know that his problem was lack of hope. He hated the idea of being average, and he could see no prospect of getting out of that category. "I couldn't see the light at the end of the tunnel. I looked at various franchise opportunities. I knew that working for a salary was not the answer, so I kept trying to find a business that would break me out of the rut, but I couldn't find one that would work for me. I couldn't afford the up-front cost of getting into anything that had any real potential."

His life was going nowhere. He was fast becoming a middle-class, white-collar corporate cliché. He drank a lot, was arrested for DUI (driving under the influence of alcohol), woke up in jail a couple of times. "I hate to admit it, but the night my daughter Beth was born, my wife had to wake me up so I could get her to the hospital; I was in a drunken stupor, and I barely knew what was going on." Bill Childers, the bright and ambitious young man from Hildebrand, North Carolina, the hometown hero who had gone off to Nebraska to play football, was sinking. "I was hitting bottom," he says.

Something important happened that turned his life around. It was a religious conversion, one of those life-changing experiences that are difficult to explain to outsiders. Childers is not a theologian and not the kind of person to bludgeon others with his religion, but he is clear and unapologetic about what happened to turn his path upward: "I got to know the Man Upstairs," he explains, "and that got my head straightened out, and things got good again."

About a year later, with the Childers' life on a different trajectory, someone convinced Bill to look at the Amway plan. He was skeptical; how could anything so good have escaped his attention for so long? But he decided, grudgingly, to do it, with a promise to work the business one night a week for six months. After that, he would reassess the situation and decide whether or not to quit.

As a final prelude to signing as a distributor, Bill and his wife attended their first major Amway event, the Yager-sponsored Free Enterprise Celebration in Charlotte. He recalls that his only reason for attending was that one of the guest speakers advertised was the pole vaulter Bob Richards, an Olympic gold medalist who was at that time a national sports hero.

"When I got there," Childers says, "I forgot all about my reluctance to attend and even about Bob Richards, to be honest. What turned me on was all the other speakers, who talked about how they had built this business, and the crowd, and the whole atmosphere. I especially remember Bill Britt. He told about how he had retired from his job and how he got up on top of his motor home wearing combat boots and jumped off on top of his alarm clock and busted that thing to smithereens as a symbol of his freedom from someone else's schedule, and that really turned me on. When I left that meeting, I was ready to do this thing!" That was Saturday night. On the following Monday, he signed up as a distributor. The ignition was immediate: 120 days later, he was a Silver producer with eleven-hundred-dollars profit for the month. "I knew if Yager could do it and Britt could do it, I could do it. I wanted to be free, and I was willing to pay the price to be free. All I was waiting for was the right vehicle, and Amway was it."

Within five years, Childers was able to quit his corporate job and become a full-time Amway leader. By that time, the loss of his salary was offset many times by his Amway income, and in the years since, he has become one of America's most successful businessmen. His organization now includes well more than one hundred thousand distributors, and his business is so wide and so deep that very few financial goals seem outside his reach.

What is so special about Bill Childers? He thinks about the question carefully: "My gift," he says finally, "is that I can honestly say, 'If I can do this, with all the dumb, ignorant mistakes I've made in my life, anybody can do it.'"

15

Trends

Some trends in the world economy today are so obvious that only an idiot could miss them.

The study of social and economic trends has become a science, and large numbers of experts in think tanks and research institutes around the globe devote their careers to the analysis of our society — where it is and where it is headed, the microtrends and megatrends, the booms and boomlets.

But some things are obvious, even to the amateur. For example: the computer is here to stay, the price of real estate is not getting cheaper, and the world population just keeps on growing — obvious things like that.

There are several trends, almost as obvious, that directly

affect the future of Amway. Whatever one's attitude toward Amway, no serious person can miss the following clear indicators that will make Amway more attractive to millions of new prospective distributors in the next decade:

1. Baby boomers need help with retirement.

2. Economies are becoming more global.

3. Corporations cut costs by cutting people.

4. The multilevel wheel has already been invented.

Baby Boomers Need Help With Retirement

We are bombarded today with news reports reminding us that the leading edge of the baby boom is now heading toward retirement; the first of the boomers, those born in 1946, celebrate their fiftieth birthday this year. Suddenly, as the biggest population group in history looks down the road toward retirement, what they see has them scared silly — they are going to need significant additional income to retire comfortably, and they are running out of time to earn it.

This is not the idle fantasy of someone trying to sponsor middle-aged people into a new business; it is the consensus of futurists. The *Boston Globe,* in a special report in April 1996, states that the boomers are "heavy on credit-card debt and short on savings." Further, they have suffered a decline in living standards and expect more from life than they can now afford. Says the *Globe,* "Boomers who reach their senior years without substantial savings or a big inheritance could face tough sledding." The report further speculates that boomers will respond to this generational crisis by finding ways to make extra income because they will be the healthiest and hardest-working generation ever.

This trend is so pronounced that the Clinton administration has planned special conferences to deal with it. Citing the fact that seventy-six million Americans are in this age group, the *Los Angeles Times* recently said the government must "devise ways to help a frightened and freaked-out baby boom generation prepare for retirement." An official with the U.S. Department of Health and Human Services says that this generation has "a pervasive sense of anxiety, because they don't have enough saved for a financially secure retirement, but feel helpless to do anything about it." This same generation is affected throughout the world, from Hungary to Hong Kong.

The pending retirement crisis creates the basis for a major movement toward opportunities such as Amway. Look at the pieces of the puzzle: millions of people, needing additional money for their futures and accustomed to hard work who have passed the most intensive period of their primary careers, will soon be seeking a way to build for the future with little capital investment.

Prediction: Baby boomers, many of whom have heard of Amway for years but have *not* been open to it, will begin looking toward retirement and will take a second, more positive look.

Economies Are Becoming More Global

The Berlin Wall is not the only wall that has come down. The walls in people's minds have begun to come down as well, and even small-town provincial mind-sets are suddenly discovering connections to people in many different countries.

The reasons are obvious: fax machines, improved travel and telephone technology, and, most importantly, the tremendous trend of corporations around the world to do business globally. Trade agreements are making international commerce easier and more profitable, and the difficulty of making a profit solely within one's own country is forcing more and more companies to think on a global basis. The ripple effect is now reaching ordinary Americans, Canadians, Australians, and so on, and the speed with which all this is happening is accelerating exponentially.

The channels of global trade at the corporate level are in place. And now, increasingly, the attitudes of the typical citizen are catching up. What is missing from this puzzle is that there are few business mechanisms by which the average person can cash in on this dramatic trend toward a global economy. Globalization may make a difference to Coca-Cola or Delta Airlines, but how can it possibly matter to an individual schoolteacher, factory worker, or housewife?

Obviously, the first companies that find a way to hook up the average person to the income/profit potential of the global economy will thrive, as people discover they can participate in the international marketplace. This single feature alone may be *the thing* that enables Amway to emerge as an international corporate giant in the next ten or fifteen years. Amway is one of the few ways available to ordinary people to tap into the success that the globalization of the world's economy produces.

Prediction: Amway's unique *system* of allowing anyone in more than seventy countries and territories to share profits from international markets will make Amway one of the primary profit centers for many people and will give it a huge new edge over its direct-sales and network marketing competitors.

Corporations Cut Costs by Cutting People

Downsizing is the current term for this trend, but there is nothing new in it. The fastest way to improve profits on the bottom line, for virtually all employers, is to reduce overhead, and the fastest way to reduce overhead is to cut payroll costs. This is a truism of corporate management.

What *is* changing is the rapid and universal spread of this practice in virtually every sector of the world's economy. Even in those occupations which have traditionally been exempt from downsizing, the ax is being sharpened, and people who have previously been thought to be untouchable are losing their jobs. An example is in education, an industry where tenure is virtually a sacred concept, guaranteeing lifetime contracts for hundreds of thousands of teachers. In a meeting of the presidents of the Council of Independent Colleges in 1996, it was reported that legislative action to eliminate tenure in American public institutions is now underway in forty-eight of the fifty states.

This action reflects a growing "nothing-is-sacred" trend that is apparent in all areas of industry, in the nonprofit sector, and in government at all levels. If a job can be done by a computer or a robot (and increasingly it can), the decision is virtually a foregone conclusion: it will. *USA TODAY,* in February 1996, devoted a special section to the sweeping changes produced by downsizing and the vast implications for a changed American society. It reported that a record 5.5 million workers, many of them white-collar, lost jobs in 1991 and 1992, a record, and that only 32 percent of them had found full-time work at equal or higher pay by 1994.

What is the solution for these millions of people and tens of millions more around the globe who feel the threat of downsizing? The growing appeal of going into business for oneself. What was considered, only a few years ago, to be an exotic and rare adventure is becoming more and more common. The *USA TODAY* report describes people who are let go from their jobs: "A key change has occurred in their beliefs: Where they once thought it was risky to start their own business, they now believe it is far more risky to work for a large corporation."

Prediction: Companies grow leaner as employers protect their bottom line but do not protect their employees.

As this trend increases, there will be a rush toward businesses such as Amway by men and women who enjoyed the status and security of good jobs only five years ago.

The Multilevel Wheel Has Already Been Invented

There is a peculiar fantasy that persists among people who are attracted to the rewards of multilevel type businesses, an illusion that might be called the "ground floor fantasy."

The people harboring this fantasy imagine that they will somehow be standing around when a wholly new business, which has all the positive characteristics of the perfect multilevel, will magically spring full-blown into existence, giving the lucky individual the opportunity to be among the first to join it. This is referred to as "getting in on the ground floor," and it is sheer fantasy.

Think about it this way: The "new world" called America could only be discovered once. It makes little sense to sit around waiting for another continent to be discovered that is "just as good as" North America but that no one else knows about, allowing the lucky individual to buy up all the land cheaply and make a fortune. This is not going to happen because there is no law of nature that guarantees that there are an infinite number of Americas just waiting to be discovered. There are not an infinite number of wheels just waiting to be invented. There are not an infinite number of Amways just waiting to be organized.

There is just one wheel, and it is so nearly perfect that one cannot improve on the basic design. So intelligent people grab it and do something with it, rather than wishing for a newer version that is somehow better than the original wheel.

One of the most obvious trends in the global marketplace is that multilevel or network-marketing businesses are hot. Very hot. Finally, after maybe fifty years of skepticism, even the economic hotshots and wise guys agree that network marketing is a powerful concept, that it is here to stay, and that it is a perfectly legal and sound way to generate significant income for large numbers of people — so long as the company, its founders, and the specific multilevel marketing plan itself is sound and the thing being marketed is a good product or service.

When something is trendy, everyone jumps on the bandwagon, and that is what has happened in recent years with multilevel businesses. A new version pops up every day. Think carefully now: Why is it that the most common way to promote any new multilevel is to describe it as "the next Amway," or "just like Amway, only better," or "just like Amway, but you can get in on the ground floor"? Obviously, Amway has become the standard against which all others are measured. Amway is the basic wheel. In what way can something new improve on it?

The ground floor is not what it is cracked up to be. Amway today is far better than it was when it was on the ground floor in 1959. It has been refined, test-marketed, and upgraded for nearly four decades. It has met its critics, honed off its rough edges, sweetened its rewards, spruced up its image, improved and expanded its products and services, and streamlined its techniques. In the brutal business environment of trial-and-error, it has made thousands of mistakes and learned from them. It is, admittedly and proudly, no longer a business that one must begin on the ground floor. In fact, one could agree that Amway creates equal ground-floor opportunities each time the company introduces a new product line.

Question: Would an ambitious student pass up a chance to go to Harvard because a brand-new college, just opening its doors, argues that there he could get in on the ground floor? Probably not. A savvy prospective student ignores GFU (Ground Floor U) and enrolls in an institution that has proven over the years that it can deliver.

Prediction: As the multilevel concept continues to gain momentum, hundreds of new start-up companies, peddling everything from panty hose to mutual funds, will sprout as fast as mushrooms and die almost as fast. Amway, having perfected its approach over a long period of time, will continue to outgrow them all.

16

Struggles

In telling the stories of Amway distributors, the tendency is to emphasize the victories and minimize the struggles.

But make no mistake about it — nothing as significant as a Diamond distributorship comes easily, and most people who get to that level overcome numerous obstacles along the way.

Portland, Maine

Consider the case of Tim and Sherri Bryan, for example. Today they lead one of the deepest and most profitable Amway businesses in all of New England. From their home in Cape Elizabeth, Maine, to their estate in Florida, they are so comfortably entrenched as leaders of a rock-solid, mature distributorship that it is difficult to imagine a time when things were different.

It appears that Amway came easily to Tim Bryan.

Nothing could be further from the truth.

When the young Yankee couple saw the business, Tim was teaching fifth grade and working a second job part-time in construction and rental real estate. When they went to a friend's house to see the plan, neither expected to be interested. They were crammed into an overheated living room and seated uncomfortably on a piano bench. Anxious to escape from the cramped environment, they left immediately after the meeting. Tim had no interest whatsoever; Sherri wondered, "What if it works?"

But their friend was persistent, so they saw the plan a second time under more comfortable conditions and cautiously decided to try it. Tim was still unenthusiastic, but they signed up and scheduled a meeting.

For that first home meeting, Sherri invited twenty-two couples, and Tim invited only one. Their disproportionate contribution to the success of the evening made no difference, however, because no one showed up, anyway. No one. Tim's batting average was zero-for-one, and Sherri's was zero-for-twenty-two.

They tried again. This time they worked together to invite nine couples but had the same result. Nobody came. Nobody.

They tried a third meeting. Again, they searched their prospect list and found nine couples to invite. Once again, absolutely no one showed up. Zero.

Finally, they found someone who would look at the circles; Sherri went to the tenant who rented their upstairs apartment and persuaded him to come downstairs and see the plan.

After that, things improved slowly, but very slowly. Tim

had every reason to conclude that he just wasn't cut out for this business. Even though he was a teacher, he taught fifth graders, and getting up in front of a group of *adults* scared him almost to the point of paralysis. As he would drive to meetings where he intended to show the plan, he was so scared that he literally became physically nauseated. Hours before every evening meeting he would be so nervous that the knot in his stomach made it impossible for him to eat lunch. This is not a good sign.

It is a whopping understatement to say the business did not come naturally to Tim Bryan, but sometime during those first few weeks he was seized by the dream of financial freedom. As a boy, he played basketball and football in high school, and his father was never able to see him play because he was at his job all the time. Tim didn't want to live that way. He had a dream of retiring from his teaching job as a young man, and however painful it was for him to talk in front of people, his dream would not die. So he persisted.

One of the wonderful things about facing this kind of paralyzing fear is that, if it doesn't kill you, it does begin to subside, and that was what happened with Tim. At some point, his natural ability to persuade and talk effectively kicked in, and things got better. He kept at it until finally he whipped the monster. "Once I got going," he remembers, "I would get so excited that I actually couldn't go to sleep at night."

Sherri was a powerful ally. While Tim was still struggling, she refused to be discouraged, even when she had to go to their first Free Enterprise Celebration alone. She was a fighter, as tough as Tim, and shrugged off her negative friends while she patiently waited for her husband to ignite. "Some of the women where I worked put me down in those early days for leaving my children at night to build the business. A few years later, they were still working, and

I was able to quit the job and be with my kids all day, every day."

There was no quit in Tim and Sherri Bryan, and finally the wall crumbled. After several months, their PV (point value) was still less than one hundred, but then suddenly it jumped to seventeen hundred the next month, then to forty-eight hundred the next month, and then to more than eight thousand the next.

They have never looked back.

Springfield, Missouri

Ken Stewart faced troubles of a different kind.

Stewart is a Midwesterner who grew up hard and made big bucks in the real estate business at an early age, then lost it all, and by the time he came into the Amway business, he was deep in debt and felt like a total failure.

Growing up in Springfield, Missouri, Stewart always knew how to work hard. He disliked high school, was expelled for a series of minor infractions ("I always seemed to be in the wrong place at the wrong time"), and joined the U.S. Army. After a tour of duty in Korea, he got an early discharge and was back in civilian clothes as a veteran by the time his classmates graduated from high school.

Ken began working on a construction crew, and within a few years began his own small construction company. By the time he was twenty-seven, he was building almost fifty houses a year and was borrowing money to keep it all going. He got overextended, was leveraged to the hilt, and just at that point, the economy soured, and interest rates skyrocketed. Soon he was living from week to week on *next* week's earnings. "I reached a point of quiet desperation. I was in an absolute rut. I got to where I didn't want to get up in the morning."

Mark Twain once observed that "the prospect of imminent death wonderfully concentrates the mind." And so it was with Ken Stewart. His young wife described the situation: "We owed three hundred thousand dollars. Ken went into a deep depression. I walked into the bedroom one night, and he was sitting on the bed crying like a baby. I was scared. I didn't know what to do for him. I knew something had to change."

It was in this condition that Ken Stewart was sponsored into Amway, and he turned to it like a drowning man to a lifeboat. It didn't let him down. Battling the stress of his mountain of old debts, he built his Amway business so relentlessly that he made Diamond twenty-four months later. The first two years were rough. He recalls the embarrassment of pleading with bill collectors to wait for their money while he summoned up the confidence to go out and show the plan each night.

Today Stewart is a Crown Direct and his days of debt and depression are a distant memory. He lives in a luxurious custom-built Western retreat where he entertains members of his group, sharing with them both the fruits of his success as well as the example of the struggles he overcame to get there.

McConnelsburg, Pennsylvania

At about the same time, in a very different part of the country, Linda Harteis was also becoming desperate, not about money, but about her marriage.

Linda and her husband Fred are both native Pennsylvanians who grew up in farming families with many children. Fred was one of fourteen children; Linda, one of eight. It is not surprising that both knew how to work hard and take nothing for granted. After they married, Fred began teaching school and Linda worked as a secretary. They had a modest lifestyle with no money left over for frills, but they were getting by.

Their crisis was not financial, but marital, and Linda felt

the stress most sharply. She describes where they were: "We were at a point in our marriage when I was wondering what Fred felt for me. When Fred and I saw the Amway business, what impressed me most was that I saw couples who cared for each other. That's all I saw. That's what turned me on about Amway. I figured if we got nothing out of it but a better relationship, it would be well worth it."

So the hardworking young couple joined the business, and the first several months were difficult. Fred and Linda Harteis had to learn to balance the demands of marriage and family with the intensity of a new Amway business. It was a challenge for their young family, but they learned that, as they focused together on a common dream with a concrete way to reach it, their marriage improved. And something else happened as well — they learned that they were extremely well-suited to the business. It rewarded their appetite for hard work and Fred's no-nonsense leadership style. Over a four-year period, they laid the groundwork for a lifetime business, left their jobs to go full-time, and eventually became Double Diamonds.

Today, the lifestyle that Fred and Linda enjoy exceeds whatever they could have imagined as a struggling young couple. The usual set of luxury items, like their Lamborghini Diablo sports car, are now merely part of the predictable possessions of people of means. But one of Fred's expensive hobbies is more unusual; he has a passion for big-game hunting and has hunted in exotic locations around the world. Hunting to Fred Harteis doesn't mean squirrels or deer in Pennsylvania anymore; the trophies on his walls could grace in the most exclusive hunting lodges on five continents. Fred and Linda Harteis found something to do together that *brought* them together, and that may have been the best payoff of all.

17

Refuse to Lose

It seems as if Tim Foley was always destined to live his life on the big screen in living color.

Things didn't begin that way for him — quite the contrary. His story begins in an orphanage in Chicago, where a loving Irish-Catholic couple named Foley, unable to bear biological children of their own, found and adopted him when he was an infant.

His adoption was the first of a string of positive events in Tim's life that continues to this day. In most respects, his childhood was like that of any kid growing up in any middle-class neighborhood in the 1950s; but it was obvious from his earliest years that he was unusually gifted in two important areas: athletics and the ability to dream.

Athletically, he seemed to do everything well. Sports of all types came naturally to him, and he enjoyed them all, though basketball and football were his favorites. His athletic skill, however, was clearly not a product of an exceptional body; he was not big or particularly fast or strong. He lacked the raw physical talent that might have impressed the casual observer, but he loved to compete, and most of all, he disliked losing. He hated to lose.

Most young ballplayers fantasize about growing up to be professional athletes, making it to the big time. The sports dreams of little boys are among the most common dreams in life. Every neighborhood playground is filled with them. But even as a child, Tim Foley was not an average dreamer; he was a world-class dreamer, a big-screen, Technicolor dreamer. His dreams were specific and detailed; they had an unusual depth and energy. When he dreamed of throwing a deep pass to the end zone to win the NFL championship or driving a fastball deep into the upper deck at Milwaukee County Stadium to win the World Series, he was creating an appetite for achievement that would sustain him through adolescence and adulthood.

When Tim reached high school, his athletic skills matured rapidly. He attended Loyola Academy, an all-boys Catholic school run by the Jesuits. There he lettered in both basketball and football. As a six-foot, 180-pound defensive back, he captained the team as a senior and led them to the Catholic league championship in Chicago. He was named to several all-star teams and was recruited by Purdue University to play college football.

When Foley arrived on the Purdue campus as a freshman, he was moving to a tougher level of competition, and he realized he was coming to the party with only average size and speed. He felt fortunate to have a shot at the team and considered his chance of ever playing pro football to be virtually nonexistent. In fact, on his freshman admission forms, he was asked the question, "What are your plans after graduation?" Young Foley wrote in reply: "To make a million dollars and get married." His answer turned out to be amazingly prophetic: he *did* get married and made a (few) million dollars, but that gets ahead of the story.

First, there was fifteen years of football to be played. Foley had a brilliant career at Purdue. In the high-pressure atmosphere of the Big Ten Conference, he thrived. He was named to the all-conference team in his sophomore season and as a senior in 1969 was recognized as one of the nation's best defensive football players. He won numerous honors, was selected to play in the college all-star game at Soldiers Field, and achieved college football's highest honor when he was appointed to the All-American team as a cornerback.

Along with the attention of the sports media his senior year, he also caught the eye of pro scouts from the National Football League. When draft day came, Foley's phone rang, and on the other end of the line was Don Shula, the famous head coach of the Miami Dolphins. "We want you," Shula was calling to say. "Your size is questionable, and your speed is questionable, but we want you to sign a contract and come to training camp, and we'll see if you can do the job."

Maybe the size and speed were questionable, but never the heart. When Tim Foley unpacked his bags at the Dolphins training camp that summer of 1970, he brought with him a fighting spirit and his fierce determination not to lose. That proved to be enough, not only for him to make the team that rookie season, but for him to become a defensive leader on what would become one of the greatest football teams of all time. The Dolphins had won only three games in a fourteen-game season the year before Foley was drafted. Within four years, the team would win back-to-back Super Bowls and make pro football history with a perfect 17-0 season, a record never matched. As an athlete, Foley was in the right place at the right time, a winner surrounded by winners, and his pro career eventually spanned eleven seasons. Along with the many team honors, Foley's career was capped by the individual honor of being selected All-Pro in 1980.

But the eleven long seasons of hitting and being hit took a toll on Foley's body. He had always been somewhat prone to injury, even in college, and as a Dolphin he had become a familiar face at Miami's Mercy Hospital. In the summer of 1981, coming off injuries from the previous season, Foley realized he would be unable to pass the physical exam to begin training camp, so he retired from the team, ending twenty-plus years of strapping on a helmet and waging war every autumn.

Now it was time to answer the question that every professional athlete eventually faces: Would there be life after football?

The answer, for Thomas David Foley, was yes — not merely yes, but a loud and emphatic YES! with a capital *Y* and an exclamation point.

Even before retiring from the Dolphins, Foley had been shown the Amway plan. He wasn't interested and paid little attention to it. He was married — to Connie, whom he had met at Purdue and married after his rookie NFL season — and had two children. They enjoyed what seemed a model upper-middle-class life in suburban Miami. He was president of a company in which he had invested heavily, a company which owned and managed health clubs. "Business was good," he explains, "but the pressure was terrific. We had borrowed almost four million dollars to build racquetball clubs in Dade County, and we were at the point that we had to sell eighty thousand dollars' worth of memberships every month to make the thing work. Sometimes I felt my business was running me, instead of my running it.

"We were doing pretty good, but the economy was uncertain. When interest rates went up, club memberships went down. We just didn't know, from one year to the next, how things were going to shake out in the health club business. I wanted an option."

That was Foley's situation when an ex-teammate from the Dolphins asked him if he would take time to look at a business opportunity. He was open to something new, but he had been approached a couple of times before about Amway, thought he knew all about it, and was sure he wanted nothing to do with it.

"Is it Amway?" he demanded to know.

And to his surprise, the answer was direct and forceful: "Yes, it is, but you need to just shut up and listen!"

When he did, the whole deal was more attractive than he thought it would be, so he agreed to consider it. In the next several days, he sought advice from people outside Amway whose opinions he respected. He half-expected them to trash the idea and was surprised when they were at least mildly encouraging. He decided to take the plunge, and the next chapter of his life began.

There were challenges right from the beginning. First, there was Foley's time problem. He still was running an active company with a demanding schedule. In addition, he worked during the football season as a sports commentator for Turner Broadcasting Network. He was on the road constantly, doing college football games across the country. During his first year in Amway, he was on the road thirty-five out of forty-five days at one point during the season. There was little time to build his Amway business.

The second challenge was the initial resistance of his wife Connie. She was not merely unexcited about Amway; she was at first downright hostile. "It took awhile for Tim's dream to become my dream," she recalls. "When we signed up, I just didn't want anything to do with it. For about six months, I was really negative and ugly. I was the kind of woman who was totally focused on my suburban life with my family. I loved being home with my children. My fear of changing my life, of stretching out to something new, was very real."

So in the beginning, Tim did it all by himself. "I literally wouldn't show up at meetings right there in my own house," Connie remembers. "I was terrified at the thought of getting up in front of even a half dozen people in my own living room to say anything, so I would just stay up in my bedroom or be conveniently gone. Tim did it all — even the products. My mother had used Amway products for about ten years before we got in the business, and I knew how good they were, but I didn't even help Tim with the products at first."

But Connie was too involved in Tim's happiness to be able to stand by and watch Tim go it alone. "He was working as president of a company, plus announcing for TBS, and still running around building the business, and I began to feel really guilty about it. Tim was working nonstop. So I started by doing the product pickup, and eventually I got involved. Even when I began helping, it was pretty much with a grudging spirit at first. I would load that Mazda station wagon down with products, and my attitude was, 'I can't believe I'm doing this for him!'"

But Connie's negative bent gradually changed, and as it did, her half of the partnership kicked in, and the Foley business gained speed. "The problem was me. I was in a comfort zone, and I had to break out of it. So I started listening to tapes, reading books, and going with Tim to functions. What has happened has been almost a miracle. This business has done wonders for our whole family, and I guess especially for me."

A dozen years later, the Foley track record is one of the most brilliant in the world of Amway. The kids, Katie and

Tommy, are virtually grown now, the family has moved from Miami to the central Florida area near Orlando, and the Triple Diamond Foleys enjoy all the luxuries that wealth provides.

As Amway Corporation opened new markets in Latin America, the Foley organization was one of the first to build significant businesses in Mexico, Central America, Argentina, and Brazil. They have been conspicuously successful in attracting other dynamic young baby-boomer couples like themselves into the business and helping them develop their own successful organizations.

For Tim Foley, life must seem fairly simple: work hard, play hard, refuse to lose, dream big, and when the rewards of victory come your way, enjoy them with the team. That philosophy, which worked so well for him in football, is still working for him in the larger arena of real life.

18

The Eyes
of a Child

Often when successful Amway distributors walk on stage to take the microphone and tell their stories, some people are missing: The children.

However exciting the story sounds from the lips of the parents, however attractive the lifestyle, there is the nagging thought that perhaps all this might look quite different through the eyes of the *child* of a deeply involved Amway family.

Of course, it is not unusual for Dad and Mom to refer frequently to their children to tell how happy they are and how many nice things they can afford, thanks to the Amway income. But if the children themselves had their turn at the microphone, what would their perspective be?

Mr. and Mrs. Amway say the kids love it, but that's not quite the same as hearing it from the kids themselves.

Remember this classic advice from author Rudolf Flesch: "Don't believe grown-ups who tell you that children love spinach."

Neither, it might be added, should one necessarily believe Amway parents who tell us how their Amway children feel about this unusual business. For that, better go straight to the source.

Meet Allyson Gurley. She is eighteen years old, pretty enough to grace the cover of a teen magazine, and a bright and appealing young woman in her sophomore year at Lee College in Tennessee. When mothers send a son off to college, their fondest wish is that he will come home someday with a girlfriend like Allyson.

She is the oldest child of John and Robin Gurley, a young Diamond couple from Georgia. In her attitudes toward life in general and Amway in particular, she is typical of the many children who grow up in homes where Amway is a serious commitment. "I love the fact that my parents are Amway distributors. I love everything about it. They have been building the business since I was a baby; it's all I know. And I just can't imagine a better life than ours."

Allyson's earliest memories are inseparably bound up in the business. "Of course there are sacrifices," she reflects, "but we make them together, and that gives us such a strong sense of shared victory when we reach our goals in the business. I have always spent a lot of evenings babysitting for my two brothers. It's not always easy for children when their parents are spending lots of time building their distributorships, but the balance is overwhelmingly positive."

One thing is sure: Being an Amway kid rarely seems to penalize youngsters' performance in school. In Allyson's case, she was an outstanding high school student and entered college as a Presidential Scholar due to her high college board scores. Traditionally, the freshman year is a tough transition time for students living away from home, and their lack of self-discipline often results in poor first-year academic performance. Not for Allyson. She racked up a perfect 4.0 grade point average in her freshman year and feels that the work habits she learned from the Amway business helped her avoid the classic freshman-year slump.

"My worst problem as a freshman has been that I miss the excitement and the atmosphere of being in a home where we are building the business. I love it here at Lee College, but I enjoy being part of my parents' dream, of our family's dream, and it is such a positive thing in my life that being away from it is tough."

Does Allyson have any regrets that her parents placed such a high priority on building a distributorship?

"None. Absolutely none. I think if parents knew what a positive impact the business can have in the lives of their children, they wouldn't worry for a minute about the long hours and the sacrifices that have to be made."

Allyson Gurley's attitude is a typical one. Talk to virtually any grown child of long-term Amway distributors, and you find a happy camper. Tiffany Kinsler, a twenty-three-year-old from upstate New York, remembers her high school years when her Diamond parents, Jim and Bev Kinsler, sometimes missed her basketball games because they were away on Amway business. "I knew what was happening, and I appreciated it. My parents always gave us the big picture; I knew they were out working for our future, and I was proud of them."

Tiffany graduated from college as a political science major, and she credits Amway with providing the financial resources that enriched her college life. "I grasped the dream my parents saw in the business," she explains. "I studied in England at Oxford one semester, for example, and never had to worry about the cost. Whatever we may have missed as kids, it was more than balanced by the rewards. I *wanted* my parents to build the business! I always gave my dad the thumbs-up when he was leaving to show the plan, because I knew he was going out there and doing it for us!"

Josh Hopper's father, Dick, built a Diamond business in Oklahoma, and Josh has a similar recollection of the impact on his high school years. "My dad was a truck driver who delivered soft drinks before he got into Amway," he says, "and I saw how hard he worked for so little payoff. So I can really appreciate what Amway has done for us." Josh had always had a dream to fly and earned his private pilot's license at the age of seventeen; today he works full-time, managing several aspects of his dad's business, and studies aviation in Arizona. He also pilots his dad's plane. "Stuff like that isn't an option for the sons of truck drivers," he says simply. "We have options we never had before."

"Ditto," says Steve Victor, a third generation Amway kid and direct distributor, whose grandparents (Joe and Helyne Victor) and parents (Jody and Kathy) both built huge Crown Direct businesses. "I grew up knowing that we could do things other families couldn't do because of the time and freedom, not to mention the money, which the business provided. Maybe my dad wasn't there all the time, but it was a point of pride. We wanted to see him go out at night because we knew he was going out to secure our future. We understood that. And we also knew that he was the *only* father who was always there to meet the bus; in fact, sometimes he was *on* the bus!"

Some Amway kids are observant enough to see the impact of Amway on not only their lives, but their parents' as well. Christine LeBlanc Henry, the daughter of Massachusetts Diamonds Al and Helen LeBlanc, was already fifteen years old when her parents joined Amway.

"I figured it was a phase they were going through and they'd get over it eventually," she recalls with a touch of irony. "But when they sold their furniture upholstery business to work at Amway full-time, I knew this was serious.

"I saw them change before my eyes. Before, they were always stressed, tired, grumpy, not much fun at all. But as they shifted their focus to the business, they were more relaxed and happy. We started to spend more time together and have fun together, and it's been that way ever since."

Carolyn Hughes Culbertson is the daughter of Roland and Molly Hughes, who built a Diamond business in South Carolina, where Roland had been a professor at the University of South Carolina. She recalls the day when her parents decided to make an emphatic commitment to Amway: "They jumped in with both feet. The first thing Dad did was sit us down and show all four of us children the plan. I was the oldest, and I was only eleven, so we didn't understand it very well, but we understood that this was a family business, and we had to work as a team." (Her sister Virginia and husband Mark are Pearl Directs, building their own business as well.)

Like the master teacher he is, Roland made the point to his children with a visual object lesson. Carolyn recalls: "One of our first goals in the business was a swimming pool. Dad took us outside and showed us where the swimming pool would be. The hole wasn't even in the ground yet, but he bought a diving board and put it in the living room; there it stayed, to remind us of our dream! We all had jobs in the business, and we knew what we were working for."

The stories of Amway kids are endless and too many to mention them all. A core theme is almost always present: teamwork, a shared dream, a family business. That basic approach pervades the world of Amway, from the newest young couple with their first child right up to the DeVos,

Van Andel, and Yager families themselves.

One of the most powerful affirmations of the rightness of the Amway approach is the enthusiasm with which the younger generation joins their parents' vision. At the corporate level, founders Jay Van Andel and Rich DeVos have already seen that their children are ready to assume the responsibilities of leadership. When health problems required DeVos to retire as president in 1993, son Dick DeVos stepped in, although he recognized the challenge of following such a legendary figure. "I will never be Rich DeVos," he said. "I will never replace or supplant him. I've got to earn my stripes. There isn't anyone alive who can replace my father, but my hope is that I'll be able to continue the same traditions and philosophy."

Like the DeVos and Van Andel families, the Yager family is engaged in a gradual changing of generations. Three of Dex and Birdie's sons now run the day-to-day operation of the sprawling InterNET Services Corporation. Jeff is president, makes most manufacturing, financial and investment decisions, and provides the overall management direction of the company, including oversight of the Yager construction and real estate companies. Doyle, oldest of the three, is chief marketing officer, publishes the InterNET magazine, and is chiefly responsible for liaison with the field distributors, tracking market trends and anticipating distributor needs. Youngest son Steve serves as senior vice president. He directs the huge area of domestic and international operations and oversees the distribution of support materials, product development, and events management.

Along with their three sisters and brother Dexter Jr., the young Yager men bring a lifetime of experience to their respective roles. What they share in common is the same attitude expressed by so many Amway kids across the country — the sense that Amway is a family business, that its successes and challenges belong to parents and children alike. Across generations, they share the work, and they share the rewards.

In families that are deeply involved in the Amway business, there seems to be no sense that Dad or Mom have a job off in an office somewhere and that the kids are detached from it, as is necessarily the case when parents are involved in conventional careers and professions. Instead, the children themselves have a sense of ownership, and that may be a critical difference.

The pervasive feeling of ownership shines through in the way Andrea Mazzeo the daughter of Frank, a former dentist, and Joan Mazzeo, recently described one of her most vivid memories: "When my parents walked across the stage as new Diamonds," she recalls, "it was one of the most emotional experiences of my life." The meaning is clear; it was not *their* achievement, but *our* achievement that was being recognized, according to Andrea, and that feeling of shared victory between parent and child may be the most important gift of all.

19

A Gallery
of Dreamers

The big auditorium is dark. The air is electric. Like magic wands, several tightly focused spotlights wave over the packed house. The room is swelling with anticipation. Huge loudspeakers blast the theme from *Rocky*. The clamor dies down slightly when the emcee, in a tuxedo, grabs the microphone. "Get ready to rummmmmmmm...bulllll!" The crowd goes crazy.

"This thrill-packed evening features possibly the two best pound-for-pound public speakers in the business and one of the finest heavyweights to ever draw a circle. This, ladies and gentlemen, is the big time. A night of champions...Jerry and Cherry Meadows are in the house"!

Cherry is dynamite. A tiny, good-looking woman, she

wows this Nashville audience with infectious enthusiasm and sets 'em up for a knockout later in the evening. Her speech has the confident air of one at peace with herself. She clearly knows who she is and what she and her partner and their business can do. Sparring with the audience, she urges them "to take no prisoners...make no apologies...fight...make it happen!" The audience erupts.

After going toe-to-toe with the scrappy lightweight champ for half an hour, the crowd is about ready for the knockout. Waiting in the wings is the heavyweight champ and love of her life, husband Jerry Meadows. This real-life Rocky has a story that will indeed blow them away.

Unlike his vivacious wife, Jerry starts slowly. He describes a time before the spotlights and crowds. A time when he and Cherry paid their dues in much smaller venues, roughly the size of the average living room. All they needed was a shot at the big time. An opportunity.

Jerry had parlayed his college degree into a plant manager's position in the textile industry. To Cherry's folks back in Michigan it had that unmistakable ring of success — manager of an entire factory of what North Carolinians called "lint heads." He now had the opportunity to work seventy to eighty hours a week for a straight salary. But when he did the arithmetic, his pay was equivalent to just pennies more an hour than the foreman. A genuine gold-plated plastic nameplate on the door was also included!

Then along came Dexter Yager.

The Meadows first met the transplanted New Yorker in a friend's living room; Yager was the one drawing circles and spinning dreams. No matter how fast Yager talked, the sophisticated college man, Meadows, was thinking way ahead of him. After five years of college and a brief stint in the corporate world, Jerry's instincts were decidedly defensive. After all, he thought, dreams are kids' stuff.

Much to Jerry's chagrin, the first person to speak after

Yager put the chalk down was his wife. He sank lower in his friend's couch when he heard Cherry's inimitable bouncy voice: "Mr. Yager, how do we get involved?"

Millionaires are not fools. Recognizing Jerry's reluctance, Yager said the magic words. The New Yorker's measured response was what Jerry would later call "a turning point." With the calm assurance of one who knows, Yager said, "Folks, this is a good idea this evening. It will be just as good tomorrow."

On the way home, the five-foot lightweight champion started softening up the big heavyweight's resistance. Light jabs at first. "Honey, this could change our lives." But Jerry was ready. He quickly responded with the two defensive lines he had practiced while still on his friend's couch. "First, it's probably illegal; and second, if it did work, it wouldn't work for us."

The lightweight countered with, "It might; it just might." Again, Jerry patiently explained that it would not work for them: "Remember, I'm a plant manager. I work twelve-to-fourteen-hour days."

Cherry wore him down by repeating, "It might, Jerry; it just might." Finally, the big guy fell, and they signed up.

Now they were ready to take on the world. After about a year in the business, the hardworking couple had only thirteen distributors and averaged $358 per month in gross sales. Wow! With almost no hard evidence that this thing really worked, Jerry and Cherry drove to Michigan to show the plan to her dad. His contacts and affable personality made him a natural for the business.

After the car was unloaded and the grandkids hugged and scrubbed and put to bed, Jerry and Cherry sat down at the kitchen table to tell the story. Before they were through the fifth circle, Cherry's normally patient and kind father pushed his chair back and had a hearty laugh at the expense of his daughter and her stunned husband (He finally quit laughing and was recruited after his daughter and son-in-law bought their first Cadillac.)

In one sense, the visit did not go well. However, there is nothing quite like adversity to force a decision. Tired of having so little to show for their efforts, and with friends and relatives questioning their sanity, the Meadows could no longer afford the luxury of mediocrity. On the long ride back to North Carolina, they made a steely-eyed commitment to a championship.

They had a newfound sense of urgency. Before the encounter in the Michigan kitchen, the Meadows' policy was a polite "show and wait" (show the program and wait for the prospects to come around). After being laughed out of Cherry's folks' kitchen, the routine was revised to "show and go." Now they were on a mission.

Jerry and Cherry had discovered the ingredient that would propel them to greatness. No, they were not there yet; they were not yet champions. But it was obvious they were going to be. They had at last discovered the will to win. They had the look — "The Eye of the Tiger!"

The champ's story has wowed the crowd. He's closing now. Wrung with emotion, their collective knees buckle under his string of eloquent word pictures and descriptions of their current lifestyle. You are there at their sprawling Tennessee estate complete with white picket fences and horses; a limousine graces the front drive. You are there as they travel to all the places they previously only dreamed of. You are there when he and Cherry watch giant waves crash against the black-rocked coast of Maine. You can smell the coffee when the sun rises over the "purple mountain's majesty." As he describes the sun sinking into the "amber waves of grain," it's almost unfair when he quotes his little boy saying, "Dad, God is a good artist!"

The big crowd is breathless. It remains only for the fictional announcer in the tuxedo to come back and declare

Jerry and Cherry Meadows "winners." But that won't be necessary. Unlike Rocky, the Meadows are real champions and very much alive.

A Couple of Extremes —
Jack and Anna Margaret "Effie" Reid

They both grew up in Winchester, Virginia, but the differences were obvious from the start. She was the mayor's "wild" daughter, and he, the son of a heavy-drinking truck driver.

As in most small Southern towns, Winchester was divided between the haves and the have-nots. Jack and his family lived on Tater Hill. Jack's mom worked outside the home and tried to hold the family together. Effie and her folks enjoyed life at the country club. Her mom and dad owned a successful floral shop.

Neither Jack nor Effie were typical examples of what their surroundings were supposed to produce. Jack was ambitious and Effie, known by her Christian name "Anna Margaret" at the club, was kind, spontaneous. Next to her high school graduation picture she had these words set to type: "Live fast, love hard, and die young and leave a beautiful memory."

She was a cute, fast-talking bundle of high energy. She talks with the urgency of a woman trying to crunch a lifetime of dreams into a half hour. Jack, on the other hand, was the football hero who knew that deliberate planning and patience were his only ticket off Tater Hill. It seemed inevitable that these two opposites would attract, much to the dismay of Effie's mother. She would not speak to Jack the entire time they dated. She finally broke her vow of silence only briefly the night the young lovers announced their wedding plans — for the next weekend. To this news, she could only repeat in unflattering tones, "I knew it...I knew it!"

A little Reid sprouted some eleven months after the tumultuous wedding. With a new baby and Jack's minimum wages spread thinly over the bills, Effie began thinking maybe Mom was right. Jack's dream had bogged down in the unexpected potholes of domestic life. Something had to be done. Jack's solution was education. He packed up his new baby Tal, a slightly disillusioned wife, and a renewed confidence in the American dream and talked his way into Virginia Tech.

Five years later, he graduated and accepted a position at a Charlotte, North Carolina, bank, some 360 miles from Winchester. By his own assessment, his new job was one of those "where you look good, smell good, and stay broke." He shoehorned his growing family into a small mobile home to cut expenses so he could pay back school loans and assorted bills. He and "Miss America," as he calls his spunky bride, fought and drank too much.

The family kept growing. When Todd was born, Tal was just starting school. Jack would pore over the books late in the evenings, and every time he did the arithmetic, the numbers would not budge. Nothing was going to change until there was more money. The bottom line was that Effie had to find a job, a proposition she was not thrilled with.

It was in this period that "Miss America" got a strange phone call. Her friend Linda asked excitedly, "Hey, have you tried S-A-8? It really works for me!" Effie had no clue what an S-A-8 was. Given her recent past, she thought her pal was talking about a funky new way to mix Scotch whiskey. Quickly, Linda explained that S-A-8 was a laundry product.

"Well, how can I get it?" Effie wanted to know.

"Not from me. I get mine from my friend Martha. She will even bring it over to your house. She's some kind of distributor," Linda replied.

To a woman desperate for money and not wanting to go

to work, a distributorship sounds promising. When Martha delivered the seven-pound box of soap, she was accosted by an excited housewife who wanted to know about openings in her line of work. Effie was surprised to learn that Martha's husband could make time to share the possibilities with Effie and Jack that very evening.

Jack did not share his wife's excitement. Before Bill showed up that evening, Jack cautioned her about getting too excited. They would not be getting involved, he assured her. Needless to say, Bill's host that evening was not Mr. Warmth. But before Bill finished the plan, the hostess was hopelessly hooked. Effie saw a way to make one thousand dollars a month. She simply could not sit still.

By the end of the presentation, Jack realized he would have trouble reining in his enthusiastic wife. When he finally got her attention, he "noticed Miss America's eyeballs rolling like a pea in a whistle." After registering his strong disagreement with Bill, Jack consented to allow her to try it. He would certainly not be interested. He was, after all, an executive finance officer.

Jack was finally roped into meeting Dexter Yager. It was clear to the young banker that Yager was doing very well. He suggested that Jack give it some time and take a second hard look at the business in three months. Jack's training and instincts had taught him that when money talks, he should listen.

Dexter (called in Jack's marker) in exactly three months. He wanted Effie and Jack to attend a rally. Jack, true to his word, took his wife and one other couple that she managed to recruit to attend the meeting in Charlotte.

Going back to the room that evening, the banker was determined to prove to his wife why the plan would not work. The genius of his scheme was that he would use her own circles to do it. He furiously drew the circles, but every time it came out making money. Finally, the filament in his light bulb flickered. "Hey, this could work!"

Effie's comeback line to her financial-whiz husband is priceless: "The only way you could be a bigger fool is to gain weight!" Sorrowfully, Jack looked at Effie and admitted, "I've been a perfect fool." To which she responded, "Honey, nobody's perfect."

By the following Monday evening Jack had his first prospect in his living room. He drew the circles and his life was changed!

In eight months, Effie and Jack exceeded Jack's income at the bank. In sixteen months, they doubled it. Two years after trying to prove why the plan would not work, Jack's income from Amway tripled his banking salary. He now had mental permission to walk away from the corporate world where Maalox and connections are equally important for success.

Chrysten, Jack and Effie's daughter, was born two years after Jack resigned from the bank. She has never known her dad to have a regular job.

Jack was promoted to assistant vice president just prior to his resigning from the bank. A colleague warned him, "Jack, you're gonna get in that business and lose everything you got." He was right. The boy from Tater Hill and the mayor's daughter did indeed lose everything that the bank money had bought them. They have always tended to the extremes. They lost their one-thousand-square-foot house and their beat-up Volkswagen. They now own properties (as in plural), a fleet of luxury cars, a motor coach, and boats of various descriptions.

The Reids have never been mediocre.

The Luck of the Draw — Scott and M. J. Michael

Scott and M. J. have it made.

They have two beautiful grown children, a large home on the river, another on the lake in Nevada, fancy cars, an income that matches most professional athletes, two housekeepers and a handyman. If that isn't enough, they get away from all this to exotic beaches and ski resorts an average of one week a month.

The natural tendency for the casual acquaintance is to jump to all kinds of wrong conclusions: They're really special, unusual; they had it all handed to them; anybody could do the business with their contacts; certainly it's easier when you're young, skinny, and good-looking.

These are common assumptions most successful people have had to deal with at some point. Rarely are these things said about people who fail. Watching the Michaels in operation, one would never guess that they have ever struggled with the twin killers of free enterprise — fear and doubt. They did.

Scott and M. J. were college sweethearts. The wedding was planned for just after graduation. Scott's brother-in-law had a business opportunity he wanted to share with the engaged couple as a way to earn extra money for the things they would need after they were married. His pitch to Scott was something like, "You want to have more of what you already got?" Looking around his bare-bones bachelor quarters and thinking about his rusted old Buick in the driveway, Scott expressed little interest in that proposition. When the brother-in-law offhandedly mentioned "freedom" as one dimension of "the dream," Scott's interest was piqued. The possibility of being liberated from the necessity of work was very appealing. Scott was "Willing to be temporarily ambitious in order to be lazy, first-class, later."

Scott, being a college man, wanted to check out the deal his brother-in-law was offering. He bounced the idea off the local voice of reason, his "know-it-all" buddy. In short order, the idea was laughingly dismissed as another one of his crazy schemes.

But time and his brother-in-law quietly persisted. In the space of months, the crazy brother-in-law and Scott's sister were driving a new Cadillac, moving into a new house, and quitting their regular jobs. To top it off, they celebrated with an extended vacation in Jamaica. Obviously, the family was watching. The laughter slowly died down with each successive move. With graduation and a wedding rapidly approaching, Scott and M. J. got very interested.

Now the credible brother-in-law's advice about getting started was actually sought. He got them involved, and they both saw the potential immediately. At this point, the tendency once again is to think the rest is history. Far from it.

After six years in the business, this "lucky" couple and their entire organization were producing only two thousand dollars a month in sales. Scott had been on the wrong side of corporate cutbacks and downsizing in a handful of jobs. They were struggling, but the low point was yet to come.

M. J. was pregnant for the second time. Their first son, Scottie, was now two. While waiting to see the obstetrician, M. J. was called aside by the nurse and told that the doctor had refused her prenatal care. It seems that the bill for Scottie was still outstanding. Excusing herself, M. J. went to the restroom and sobbed.

After attending an Amway convention, Scott vowed to his young wife that they would build a successful business. He had made a decision. Given their track record over the last six years, skepticism was clearly in order. But somehow M. J. believed his rash claims. For the first time she recognized a different kind of confidence in her husband's bold new visions of their future. The basic building blocks in the foundation of their dreams were simple faith and determination.

Scott and M. J. declared their independence in May of 1976. However, like a more famous Independence Day (July 4, 1776), all it really meant was that they were now ready to pay the price for total freedom. It meant all-out war!

Following hard on the heels of their declaration were several skirmishes with their formidable enemies of fear and doubt. They acknowledge that a few battles were lost. But with an uncommon faith and a gritty determination, they stood their ground. Eventually their persistence paid off, and they won the war. They have now been Diamonds for more than a decade, and all the struggles are clearly worthwhile.

Some people might think Scott and M. J. are very lucky. They know better.

Promises to Keep — George and Ruth Halsey

George and Ruth are hard workers who, in her words, "have come from a great distance." The fleet of expensive automobiles parked in their recently expanded garage is clear evidence of the impact of a considerable work ethic unleashed in a free enterprise system.

George was a quiet, shy kid who grew up in a working-class neighborhood in downtown Wilmington, North Carolina. A short bike ride away was the beautiful Atlantic coast and another world. The yachts docked in the harbor and luxurious ships sailing just off the coast caught the young boy's fancy and became the stuff of his dreams. Somehow, the young black kid on the beat-up old bicycle could see himself commanding one of these sleek sailing vessels. He had big dreams and a powerful imagination.

His mother's advice was simple and direct. She explained that tickets to this "other world" were issued only at the university. So he packed his dreams up along with his bike and a saxophone and enrolled at North Carolina A&T. For the next few years, George dry-docked his nautical ambitions and concentrated on his books and band, eventually becoming president of the marching band.

On a football game Saturday in early November, the first of

many dreams in his remarkable life came true. The beautiful head majorette missed the bus for an away game and had to ride with the band. The only vacant seat left on the crowded band bus was the one next to the grinning Halsey.

He was far too bashful to initiate conversation on campus, but this was different. Now the best-looking girl he had ever seen, and one he had admired from a distance, would be a captive audience for the next few hours. The shy young man from Wilmington started a conversation with his seat partner that day that would last a lifetime.

During their passionate courtship, George made solemn promises to Ruth's father that he would provide only the finest for his daughter. But love was impatient. Against the caution of their parents, George and Ruth were married and left school lacking his degree and her father's consent to marry.

Ruth, however, had completed her degree in physical education and modern dance before they married. Over the course of eighteen years in the local school system, the always graceful Ruth became a fixture at community social events in the Greensboro area. She was connected. As a professional in the community and a role model for aspiring young African American women, Ruth's widening circle of friends included the shakers and movers of Greensboro. Her lifestyle required a standard of living that became increasingly expensive.

George had promises to keep. Leaving college without a degree forced the soft-spoken newlywed to take work where he could find it. This dreadful series of jobs ranged from a line worker in a mattress factory to a stock clerk in a shoe store to a box maker in a pajama factory. A second job as a night janitor helped provide his gorgeous young wife a few more of the things *he* thought she needed. Ruth was grateful and supportive but continually encouraged her hardworking husband to dream bigger. "You can do better," she would whisper late in the evening.

Finally there was an opening in the Greensboro Police Department. The robust rookie officer was assigned to the toughest neighborhood beat. On Market Street, George earned a reputation as a no-nonsense officer who did little talking. He quickly gained the respect of both the local residents and the thugs.

One evening after a particularly physical arrest of a sullen drunk, George came home to change his uniform. Ruth was horrified at the sight of her blood-spattered sweetheart standing in the hallway. George's assurance that it was not his blood did little to calm her. Again, late that evening, she whispered, "You can do better."

With Ruth's encouragement and a renewed confidence in his own abilities, George checked out an opening as a claims adjuster in a local insurance company. Both George and the company liked what they saw. George left the police department and changed suits. He was issued a company car (this one had no writing on the sides nor lights on the top) and went to work with a briefcase instead of a pistol. He looked good.

After working in a world that measures time in nine-to-five increments and calculates worth in profitability statements, the Halseys appeared to be the very models of success. But slowly they were becoming victims of their climb up the social ladder. The lifestyle of the crowd they socialized with was becoming too rich for a teacher and a mid-level insurance executive. Their appearances were expensive, and they quietly struggled to keep them up. Then, almost by accident, they discovered Amway.

A friend came over to buy George's used motor home but steered the conversation around to a business opportunity. (Note: This practice is discouraged by Amway and InterNET.) George listened intently. The more he looked at the circles, the better they looked. He was hooked immediately. Ruth, however, did not share his excitement. Selling soap was not quite what she had in mind — after all, what would her high-class friends think? That night she whispered again, "George, you can do better."

Ruth knew too well that they needed extra money. For the first time, she tried to discourage her excited husband. Ironically, she had seriously prayed for God to work a financial miracle in their lives, but the one she had in mind certainly was not Amway.

For the first time, George saw a way to fulfill the promises he had made two decades earlier. If what he saw in the circles was correct, he might even uncork that silly sailing dream that he had almost forgotten.

At the end of his third week in the business, George went to a rally to learn more about the big picture and persuaded a reluctant Ruth to go along. Good thing. For the first time, Ruth saw how this plan might really work. On the way home from that Nashville meeting, the partners agreed to pool their considerable resources and expand their lifelong partnership to include their work world.

Together they were a formidable pair. George learned the plan quickly. Running on sheer excitement, they packed their basement out several times a week, and George sweated through the plan with anyone who would listen. The excitement and crowds seemed to feed on each other. The pace was frantic, and the sense of urgency was almost tangible. Barely a month in the business, George and Ruth and their people sponsored 130 people in one evening alone. Their infectious enthusiasm spread through their entire organization, energizing everyone it touched. "Sleep," he would tell his people, "was on back order."

As George drew the circles, Ruth counted the money. They quickly piled up a series of pins — Silver, Pearl, and Emerald — indicative of their accomplishments. For the first time, Ruth thought seriously about getting rich, really rich.

But strangely, the thought seemed almost hollow. She and George were discovering an economic truth that would eventually propel the two to a financial status unheard of in even their circles: the secret to fulfillment and wealth was in building successful people. This slight shift in focus from their own bank account to others' achievements propelled them to a Diamond distributorship after less than five years in the business.

Their hard work has finally afforded them the ability to live out a lifetime of delayed dreams. To celebrate their promotion to Diamond, George gave the former prancing majorette a hunk of the Diamond bonus and told her to spend it any way she wanted. Ruth went downtown and peeled off a string of hundred-dollar bills from the wad to pay for a beautiful full-length mink coat. George took the other half of the bonus and surprised her with a rare Excalibur sports car all wrapped up in a pretty ribbon. He had promises to keep.

As you can probably imagine, George (Admiral) Halsey finally got his sailing ship as well. The serious little boy from the Wilmington neighborhood always did have big dreams and a powerful imagination. The couple's Amway track record has been an inspiration for countless numbers of people. They are truly pioneers, earning the distinction of being the first African Americans to achieve all of the higher level achievements, all the way up to Triple Diamond.

Real People — Jerry and Peggy Boggus

In a makeshift stall on a Ukrainian street corner, I once saw a young Oriental man sitting behind a tall stack of brand-new jeans. The obviously hand-lettered sign advertised genuine American Buck Roger jeans. They were clearly a bad knockoff, but people were lining up to spend rubles they did not have. The important thing was that the jeans looked like the genuine article, but like most fakes they would not last. Unfortunately, genuine people are as rare as a pair of genuine Levis at a Ukrainian market.

It does not take long to understand that Jerry and Peggy Boggus are the genuine article. What you see is what you get. Even their unpretentious flat Southern accents have the unmistakable ring of truth. They have truly been there and done that and bought the T-shirt to prove it.

They are as refreshingly honest about the ups and downs of married life as they are about the secrets of their success, and they are willing to share both. One suspects, however, that the secret to both is wrapped up in a word that inevitably creeps into most of their conversations — *relationships*. Their story is full of prime examples.

As the wife of a struggling graduate student, Peggy became an expert at managing a low-income budget and a high-octane husband. She learned how to stretch a pound of hamburger meat and make her own clothes and when to back off in a disagreement — all excellent survival skills.

These skills would come in very handy when Jerry joined the U.S. Army and the small family moved to Fort Bragg, North Carolina. Uncle Sam provided the small family, Jerry and Peggy and their three children — with a small three-bedroom duplex with Army issue white walls and slate gray floors. Even with Uncle Sam paying most of the bills, the young family was just breaking even. There was precious little left over at the end of the month for pleasure. The crowded, drab apartment did little to lift their spirits. One of Jerry's old buddies from high school called one evening. He wanted to speak with Jerry, who was out of town on Army business. Peggy took the call. The friend said that he was developing an Amway business and wanted to share it with them. Peggy patiently explained that they had already seen the plan twice before and were not interested; Jerry was just too busy with his career as a biochemist in the military.

A few days later, the friend called again, and this time Jerry was home. After his buddy went through roughly the same spiel, Jerry confirmed his wife's hunch. Undaunted, the friend said, "Listen, Jerry, you haven't seen it from me. Give me one chance and take a good look. If you don't like it, I'll never mention it again." The seriousness in his friend's voice and his "dead-dog honesty" piqued the young captain's interest.

Within the week, he showed the plan to Jerry and Peggy. When he opened the door, Jerry knew something was definitely up. The old friend was decked out in a coat and tie and a major-league smile. It was clear that he was on to something.

As he drew the circles that evening, he asked Jerry and Peggy about their personal lives: "What do you dream about?" They were stumped. They could think of nothing. They had a certain kind of status, but even that was borrowed from the government. The question haunted them. After jumping through the hoops at graduate school, they had loaned their lives and their dreams to Uncle Sam. Personally, they had no particular place to grow to and no dream to pull them along.

The old friends talked deep into the night. Something stirred in the young Army couple that seemed almost dead. There were things in life that they wanted for their family, but they seemed so far-fetched, so out of reach. When it was time for good-byes at the end of the evening, the friend looked Jerry in the eye and solemnly declared, "I'm going to do this whether you do it or not." That motivational line was not necessary — the decision was made to begin, and very soon Jerry and Peggy were hooked, energized by the reawakening of long dormant dreams that now seemed possible.

For the next few months, the tiny Boggus apartment was a buzz of activity. In eight months they became direct distributors, which had a slight downside; Amway products were now all over the house. Every spare nook and cranny in the little apartment became usable space to build their growing business. The frantic pace and the constant flow of people through their apartment further fueled their dreams. The distant dream a few months ago of a larger house was suddenly becoming more and more realistic.

As the activity increased, excitement doubled. Their network of friends continued to widen. At the time, they were too busy to notice a developing pattern which they are now quick to point out — as they got better and better at building relationships with people, their business volume increased dramatically and their marital difficulties decreased significantly.

After making Diamond, Peggy paused long enough to catch her breath and evaluate what she had learned in building a highly successful Amway business. Her Top Ten list in no particular order is included below.

1. You can buy a clean house...later (if you work hard enough).

2. Be real, genuine, different. The world is tired of fakes.

3. You have to be a good listener. People flock to anyone who will hear them out. Usually at the bottom of no is a real sense of fear.

4. It is lonely at the top. Not everyone will be excited about your success.

5. Diligently practice the principle of giving both time and love.

6. You are as happy as you want to be. Happiness, like the part in your hair, is a choice. You do not have to be jerked around by circumstances. The

good news is you are in charge. If you don't like it, change it.

7. Put others first.

8. Think long term; be a "long-ranger."

9. Believe in people, and help people believe in themselves. Help them recapture that childlike faith that they can indeed sing and dance and succeed.

10. Dream as if your life depends on it!

This advice was not copied from a thick book of platitudes but gleaned from a life of real success. Peggy and Jerry have truly "been there and done that." As the poet John Keats observed more than a century ago, "Nothing ever becomes real till it is experienced; even a proverb is no proverb till your life has illustrated it."

Free as Country Sunshine — Ron and Toby Hale

Ron and Toby Hale are comfortable.

They're financially secure, to be sure, but more importantly, they are comfortable to be with. Easy. The depth of their personal honesty and the ease with which they laugh at themselves disarm the listener. It is easy to understand why even total strangers are charmed by Toby's melodious mountain accent or Ron's warm, rich baritone.

Though they shouldn't be, the Hales seem genuinely surprised at their tremendous success in the world of business. Their meteoric rise was never in the plans of these two self-defined hillbillies. The good life for these two from a "holler" of the Blue Ridge Mountains in Virginia was a simple house with the plumbing indoors and the pets outdoors. They were raised to appreciate two fundamentals of mountain life — simplicity and freedom.

For an Appalachian boy fresh out of high school, a career in the military sounded exciting. The Air Force recruiter had little trouble signing up the young man with stars in his eyes and love in his heart. Before he left the valley for the wild blue yonder, the tall gangly boy married a local coal miner's daughter.

At seventeen, Toby Ann (proper mountain girls always have two names) kissed her new husband good-bye. In a few weeks, he was shipped overseas to England. With the money they had saved, Toby Ann left Abington, Virginia, one morning on a Greyhound bus headed to the big city — New York, New York. There she boarded the *Queen Mary* for the seven-day voyage to England.

Contending with travel jitters and an angry sea, Toby was slightly more than lovesick. Clearly, the young mountain girl never found her "sea legs." When the ship docked, Ron was waiting. Nothing cures a bad case of seasickness like the sight of a six-foot-four-inch young man in a crisp, blue uniform.

In short order, Toby was pregnant and delivered their first child in a military hospital in England. After Ron was reassigned to the United States, a second and third child arrived, and their tiny base housing quarters were getting a little tight. Something had to give, but Ron's $150-per-month check severely limited the options.

In retrospect, they believe that God was listening when orders came through for Portsmouth, Virginia. That's where they met Amway.

One Friday evening about 6:30, Ron kissed Toby good-bye and told her he was going to a "business meeting." That's all he knew about it. When he was not home by midnight, Toby began to worry. By 2:00 A.M. the worry had progressed to a slow boil. When Ron finally came bouncing through the door at 2:30 grinning wildly, Toby was hot. Before she could get to her rolling pin and iron skillet, Ron picked her up and swung her around. All he could say was, "Just stay with me Toby Ann. We're gonna be rich! We're gonna be rich!" They mutually agreed to talk about it in the morning.

Ron had his wife up early the next morning. The first thing he did was insult her Tide. "For the last eleven years, Toby Ann, you've been washing my underwear all wrong!" (A remark like that does not sit kindly with a professional homemaker.) Frantically, he went from room to room looking for inferior household products. Toby finally grabbed her wide-eyed husband and insisted on some kind of explanation.

Eventually, he calmed down long enough to get Toby to a meeting where someone could explain the plan. At the end of that meeting, a plan was hammered out between the partners: Toby was to do all retailing and phone calls, and Ron would draw the circles.

For the first few months, they built a thriving business on sheer excitement. They were flying high, talking to and sponsoring neighbors, friends, family, and eventually the family doctor.

After eight months in the business, they stalled at the direct distributor level. The excitement had waned slightly after they quickly achieved their initial goal, extra income. They desperately needed a dream tune-up.

They contacted Dex and Birdie Yager, who agreed to come do a meeting. Ron and Toby rented a large junior high school auditorium, made the coffee, and waited for hundreds of people to show up. When the show finally got rolling, there were exactly sixty-eight people rattling around in the enormous auditorium.

That evening a valuable lesson was learned. Yager patiently explained to the Hales that they had to do two things. First, he said, expand your vision. Second, use proven methods of doing the business. In short, listen to your Diamond. After this complete overhaul of their thinking, Ron and

Toby began, almost immediately, to break new directs. They were finally on their way.

At thirty-three, Ron Hale retired from the Air Force. In less than four years, Ron and Toby's business grew to the point that he no longer had to depend on Uncle Sam for a living. To voluntarily walk away from a military career after almost fourteen years of distinguished service one had to have something serious to go to or a slightly loose screw. Ron is clearly not a dummy.

On the morning after he retired, he got up early again. This time he went out on his porch to watch his neighbors, who had laughed at him in the early days, go off to work. A few days later, he went downtown and bought a shiny new Cadillac. That afternoon, he called his neighbors over and cranked up his "soapbox Cadillac." He wanted them to "hear it bubble." Living well is indeed the best revenge.

Free to Fly — Jim and Dinah Martin

Dr. Jim Martin was one of Kentucky's tallest and finest veterinarians. At six feet five inches and 250 pounds, Jim commands a sense of presence and exudes an affable country charm. From his thriving practice in eastern Kentucky, "Doc" saw it all: from a two-thousand-pound ugly bull with a bad case of pneumonia, to a prissy poodle with bad breath, to a large, sullen snake with a bellyache.

Martin's stall-side manner and effectiveness with large animals helped spread his reputation as a horse doctor. One would expect a good horse doctor in the Bluegrass State to be very busy. He was.

Jim Martin had spent twenty-one years in school to earn the privilege of doctoring prize thoroughbreds and nursing blue ribbon bulls through pneumonia. In the last seven years of medical school, he ran bills that went into six figures. Upon graduation, he borrowed another hundred grand to set up a practice that included everything from a

169

cat thermometer to a portable X-ray machine. His brand of medicine required a major commitment in both dollars and time.

Veterinarians indeed make house calls, or, more accurately, barnyard calls. Obviously, pregnant mares and sick bulls do not confine their emergencies to normal business hours. Anxious farmers, like expectant fathers, are poor at playing the waiting game. They are very impatient. Needless to say, a young vet misses a lot of family dinners.

While Jim built his expanding practice, Dinah stretched the dollars at home. Jim's version of how he met his industrious young bride sounds suspiciously like an old country song. "There was a farmer in LaFollette, Tennessee, that had a bunch of pretty young daughters. I went down there and got the pick of the litter."

If one were to design a professional wife, Dinah would be the model. She and Jim were married while he was still in school. To support her husband's education, she sold a wide variety of things door-to-door, merely to raise enough money to pay the rent on the trailer. She and Jim had small dreams and big bills.

Eventually, Jim graduated. To celebrate, Jim threw all her door-to-door sales kits and catalogs in the trash. As Jim explained, "After all, you are now a doctor's wife." They soon found out that titles and status did not pay the bills. The stress of continuously generating enough capital to cover college loans, the enormous start-up cost of a medical practice, and the needs of a growing family began to take its toll. The pressure was beginning to boil over at home more frequently now.

Dinah heard about Amway. It became clear to her that Amway may be an answer for their growing financial needs. It certainly did work for all of those on the tapes she listened to.

Her favorite tape stars were a professional couple like

themselves, Tom and Carolyn Payne of Guntersville, Alabama. She "really believed Jim could identify with Tom [a dentist] if he would just listen to him."

On the way home from a conference in southern Alabama, Dinah asked Jim, "How far out of the way is Guntersville?" "A couple of hours," he replied. "Why?" Sheepishly, Dinah launched into a halting explanation that her business heroes lived there.

Jim decided to prove once and for all that the dream she was chasing was a hoax. "Dinah," he thought, "was badly deceived. Nobody could really live like they say on those silly tapes." So to prove his point, he turned off Interstate 59 and headed west toward Guntersville.

At a pay phone in the KMart parking lot in Guntersville, the spunky Dinah jumped out of the car and dialed the number. "It wouldn't hurt anything if we just called to say hello," she explained.

To her amazement, Carolyn Payne actually answered the phone and insisted that the two come over for coffee. Watching from the car, Jim quickly recognized his wife's grin and ultimately knew where this was heading. Using hand signals, he insisted that they get back on the road and quit wasting time. Carolyn continued to urge them to "please drop by for just a minute."

Tom and Carolyn were waiting in the driveway and graciously welcomed Jim and Dinah to their sprawling estate. While Carolyn and Dinah talked, Tom showed Jim around. Throughout the tour of the property, Jim was quietly cataloging the real "toys" that Tom and Carolyn's success had provided. Best of all, Tom no longer had to practice dentistry to afford them. After twenty-one years of school and a half hour with Tom, Jim was slowly getting the point of the free enterprise system. Was it possible that he could build a future on an investment of less than sixty dollars and some training?

THE DREAM THAT WILL NOT DIE

On the way back home from Tom and Carolyn's, Jim conceded. He would give "Dinah's little deal" an honest shot. "Hey, crazier things have happened." He borrowed a bunch of folding chairs from Wray's Funeral Home and set up his first big "opportunity meeting" in the spacious confines of his kennel. It was a strange setting for the dawn of a new business.

A few years later, Dr. Martin retired from the practice of veterinary medicine. Dinah personally wrote his retirement announcement and published it in the local paper. In less than forty words, this declaration of independence summed up the essence of the Amway business for the Martins and many other families hankering to be free. Dinah wrote simply:

> On the sixth day of August, Dr. Jim Martin will retire at the age of twenty-nine. He will be sharing his formula for freedom as he travels with his wife and family throughout the United States.

With these words, the Martin's cage door was forever opened. Jim and Dinah were free to travel as far as their rejuvenated dreams and a brand-new motor home would carry them. It turned out to be quite a distance. Today they live on a sprawling estate of their own complete with their entire family. Both Jim's and Dinah's parents have separate homes on the property, in addition to homes for their three children: John, James, and Joe.

Epilogue

A dream can be a fragile thing.

Dreams are such natural expressions of the human spirit. They arise easily, with little effort, from the heart, but they can also die just as easily as they are born.

The most fragile dreams are spun in thin air. They are like dainty, floating bubbles, beautiful and colorful, but unable to withstand the slightest bump of reality. They are little more than wishful thinking. And even those dreams that are noble and well-conceived can be killed by criticism or failure. These are the dreams called "might have been"; they begin bravely but wither and die when challenged by a hostile environment.

The world of direct selling and network marketing has

been the graveyard of countless dreams in the last half century. Dreams spring up overnight but die and disappear at the first onslaught of adversity.

Amway began as a dream, and after almost four decades one thing is clear: it is a tough and resilient dream. The dream was that of bringing to millions of people around the world the power to create for themselves true financial freedom. Rich DeVos and Jay Van Andel started with that simple dream; men like Dexter Yager embraced it; and it has now been tested, measured, challenged, and tried. The verdict is inescapable: it is a dream that will not die.

Amway is so well-engineered, so charged with hope and human energy, that it survives adversity and outlasts criticism. It attaches itself to men and women of faith and courage and becomes stronger as they become stronger. It shrugs off clones and wanna-bes, copycats and look-alikes, and just-as-good-as knock-off versions. It learns from its mistakes. It reinvents itself. It meets its critics in the arena, feasts on their bones, and grows in the process.

Physical trauma cannot kill this dream; ask Nancy Wilson. Mike Wallace and *Sixty Minutes* can't kill it; ask Dexter Yager. Personal loss and tragedy cannot knock it out; ask Helen Huebner. A slow start won't cripple it; ask Tim Bryan. Language barriers and national boundaries can't stop it; ask the Gulicks or the Foleys. Lawsuits don't kill it; negative reporters can't stop it; recession and inflation and high taxes can't make a dent; dropouts and no-shows don't even slow it down.

It is the dream that will not die.

Hundreds of thousands of men and women around the world have confirmed its ability to deliver on its original promise. Many people and companies have entered the multilevel arena, all of them bold and confident at the outset. Most have failed, some have prospered, but throughout the world, Amway has emerged as the standard against which all others are now compared. It has faced the mine-field of hazards and challenges that faces every creative new vision in the global marketplace and has not only survived, but grown steadily stronger.

Nobody understands dreams as the men and women of Amway do — maybe because Amway itself is the most vibrant and indestructible dream of all. Carried in the hearts and hopes of people around the world, it has proven to be a dream that will not die.

For more interesting insights into the Amway experience,
read these earlier books by Charles Paul Conn,
available in paperback by Berkley:

The Possible Dream

and

Promises to Keep

These Berkley titles, along with other books by Charles
Paul Conn and various leading motivational authors, can be
ordered from:

InterNET
12201 Steele Creek Road
Charlotte, NC 28241